The
Fifth
Freedom

Rob and Rod,
The good work you do in
the communities you serve make
you "producers" of health in
the language of this book.
Thank you for making the
world a more cared-for, inclusive,
and healthier place!
    all the best,
    Daniel Erickson

The
Fifth
Freedom

Guaranteeing
an Opportunity-Rich
Childhood for All

DAVID J. ERICKSON

BROOKINGS INSTITUTION PRESS

Washington, D.C.

Published by Brookings Institution Press
1775 Massachusetts Avenue, NW
Washington, DC 20036
www.brookings.edu/bipress

Co-published by Rowman & Littlefield
An imprint of The Rowman & Littlefield Publishing Group, Inc.
4501 Forbes Boulevard, Suite 200, Lanham, Maryland 20706
www.rowman.com

86-90 Paul Street, London EC2A 4NE

The Brookings Institution is a nonprofit organization devoted to research,
education, and publication on important issues of domestic and foreign
policy. Its principal purpose is to bring the highest quality independent
research and analysis to bear on current and emerging policy problems.

Composition by Westchester Publishing Services
Typeset in Adobe Caslon Pro

British Library Cataloguing in Publication Information Available

Library of Congress Cataloging-in-Publication Data Is Available

ISBN 978-0-8157-4003-2 (cloth)
ISBN 978-0-8157-3963-0 (pbk. : alk. paper)
ISBN 978-0-8157-3964-7 (ebook)

To my mother, Mary Ruth Erickson, whose lifelong commitment to the Social Gospel has been a North Star for my career in community development.

Contents

Preface

THIS BOOK IS THE CULMINATION of a thousand conversations with a hundred friends who have been fellow travelers in the effort to find smarter and more effective social welfare policies that do a better job of taking care of our neighbors and fellow citizens. The conversation started with my husband, Doug Jutte, almost two decades ago. We edit each other's writing, and as a medical doctor and public health professor, he tried to convince me that the work I did in antipoverty policy and finance had health implications. Like many, in those days when I heard "health" I thought "medical care." It took a long time to unlearn that; health is a bigger concept than simply the absence of disease, and he was a good teacher.

The conversation expanded to include his friends in the Robert Wood Johnson (RWJ) Foundation's Health and Society Scholars program and my friends working in the community development finance field. I am grateful to S. Leonard Syme, Nancy Adler, Kaja LeWinn, Lia Fernald, Jodi Halpern, and Tom Boyce at UC Berkeley and University of California, San Francisco for teaching me about the social determinants of health. I am grateful also to many community development finance friends, colleagues, and mentors who saw the value in a partnership between community development and health, including Nancy Andrews, Ellen Seidman, Lisa Richter, Terri Ludwig, Laura Choi, Scott Turner, Penelope Douglas, Will Dowling, Tyler Norris, Annie Donovan, Carolina Reid, Alan Berube, Paul Brophy, Raphael Bostic, Andrea Levere, Antony Bugg-Levine, Audrey Choi, Bill Burckart, Kirsten Moy, Otho Kerr, Bechara Choucair, Ruth Salzman, Ela

Rausch, Doug Shoemaker, Dan Nissenbaum, Rosa Lee Harden, Kevin Jones, Kimberlee Cornett, John Moon, Carol Naughton, and Maggie Super Church. The colleague who contributed most to this book is my friend Ian Galloway, who was first to arrive at many of the ideas I have tried to explain, including "the market that values health."

Our first efforts to bring the world of population health together with community development and antipoverty practitioners appeared in a journal issue in 2009, followed by a convening on the topic at the Federal Reserve's Board of Governors headquarters in Washington, D.C., in July 2010.[1] RWJ was our close partner, especially Elaine Arkin, Jim Marks, and, later, Don Schwarz and Amy Gillman. The then president of RWJ, Risa Lavizzo-Mourey, had the best line on this newly emerging partnership of sectors: "We are likely to look back at this time and wonder why community development and health were ever separate industries."[2] The Federal Reserve and RWJ have held over fifty meetings in the Healthy Communities series in big cities and small towns across the country. This book is an effort to capture and synthesize many of the ideas from those meetings.

Over the years that partnership between health and community development grew, and now many billions of dollars are coinvested by hospitals and Community Reinvestment Act–motivated banks, health insurers, affordable housing developers, and the like. We have made great progress, but it has not been fast enough for most of us. I hope this book helps speed the evolution.

So many people helped in the writing of this book. Thanks to an exceptional high school English teacher, Fares Sawaya, I was able to find a voice and overcome a fear of writing. His guidance was the epitome of what I refer to in the book as an airbag intervention in my life.

This book is in many ways a continuation of my first book on the history of community development and affordable housing finance policy, *The Housing Policy Revolution*. That book was based on my dissertation, where many Berkeley professors and classmates guided me—especially my adviser, Richard Abrams.

I am grateful to the Federal Reserve System, my employer over the last seventeen years, because it is an institution where data and getting to the truth, to the extent that we can, matter. I am particularly thankful to the Federal Reserve Bank of New York; its mission statement is to foster an economy that works for "all segments of society." All Americans should be proud that their central bank is staffed by dedicated public servants who take this mission seriously and work diligently to both support the economy and find ways to overcome obstacles so that all can participate in—and benefit from—an economy that works for all. And, to ensure that there is no conflict of interest with this project and my work at the Federal Reserve, I should mention that I do not benefit financially from the sale of this book. And the views I express are my own, and do not represent the Federal Reserve Bank of New York or the Federal Reserve System.

So many friends and colleagues gave great advice or read this manuscript, including Carolina Reid, Shamus Roller, Mollyann Brodie, Lisa Chamberlin, Laudan Aron, Karla Erickson Peterson, Summer Peterson, Margaret Pugh O'Mara, Suzanne Delbanco, Christopher Ojeda, Jennifer Tescher, Jack Shonkoff, Neal Baer, Nathaniel Counts, Alan Berube, Neal Halfon, and Peter Long. Readers in Hawaii, including Amy Asselbaye, Rachael Wong, David Derauf, Michael Epp, and Puni Jackson, were especially helpful in guiding an outsider to write about an amazing and complex place.

I appreciate all the advice, but the errors herein are my own.

This book is dedicated to my mother. I am sorry that she didn't live long enough to see it published. I printed out the dedication page and brought it to her in the hospital shortly before she passed away in 2019. She wasn't able to read at that point, so I read it to her. I apologized for not having finished it earlier. (She was still a little miffed that I had dedicated my first book to my husband instead of to her.) Her reply was, "Don't worry, I'll find it when it's done." She had an empathy that was remarkable. She brought that to her family, to her friends, and to the larger society that she hoped to make better. I am very lucky to have been warmed in the glow of that light, and, wherever she is, I hope she is reading this now.

Introduction and Summary

Better Policies and Improved Neighborhoods Can Secure the Fifth Freedom—an Opportunity-Rich Childhood for All

THE STATUS QUO IN THE UNITED STATES is stupid, unfair, and expensive. As a country, we spend too much on downstream consequences of people living in poverty. It is in our power to fix this problem. Rather than spending trillions of dollars on avoidable consequences, this book is an argument to spend that money on the upstream conditions that could guarantee an opportunity-rich childhood for all. A strong foundation in childhood is the best predictor of a healthy and productive adulthood and could save trillions of dollars on avoided chronic disease, incarceration, educational failures, and lost productivity.

The title of this book is "The Fifth Freedom"—a play on President Franklin Roosevelt's antifascist rallying cry, The Four Freedoms, which referred to freedom of speech, freedom of worship, freedom from want, and freedom from fear. The fifth freedom draws on an essay written by UC Berkeley researchers, titled "Social Dominance, School Bullying, and Child Health."[1] In that essay, Halpern and colleagues argued that all children have a right to an "open future," borrowing from the language of antibullying ideas from the American philosopher Joel Feinberg. The obligation rests in the relationship parents have with the state that requires their children to attend school. This relationship works because schools are committed both to protecting children from harm

1

(e.g., bullying) and to "nourishing the child's future opportunities." The authors conclude, "Society thus makes a promise, assuming responsibility for promoting each child's right to a reasonably open future."[2]

The fifth freedom, a freedom to an open future, is a commitment that all children will have the conditions and tools to thrive—not just in school, but at home and in their neighborhoods. They should not be bullied by peers, family, the conditions in their neighborhoods, or the larger society. The fifth freedom sounds like an overly broad concept and amorphous promise, but the strategies to make sure it happens are concrete: guardrails and airbags.

Guardrails are the aspects of a well-functioning neighborhood that nudge and guide us to build the skills needed to thrive in adulthood—good schools, well-funded libraries, safe streets and public spaces, quality health care, spiritual homes (churches, etc.), and well-functioning transportation that puts other essential amenities in reach, especially jobs. Airbags, on the other hand, are critical interventions at the individual level; they are interventions that are timely and help avoid the long-lasting damage that can follow from a bad event. This idea was first articulated by Harvard professor Robert Putnam, who wrote about it in his book, *Our Kids*.[3] Examples of social airbags are drug treatment after a person is rushed to a hospital for a drug overdose, or psychological counseling for a young person exhibiting signs of severe depression. We have enough money and know-how to make sure all children have both guardrails and airbags, so that they are in a position to develop into healthy and productive adults who become effective parents for the next generation.

In short, I am arguing for a reimagination of a smarter social safety net. The Hollywood movie pitch is this: *Catcher in the Rye* meets blockchain technology. The main character in that book, Holden Caulfield, wanted to keep children safe, and blockchain allows for smarter case management among multiple service providers over the life course. Just as Holden wanted to be the one in the rye field who caught the children whose height didn't allow them to see the cliff they were racing toward, the new approach to a smarter social safety net will catch kids heading in the wrong direction before they can be harmed.

In many ways, this book is motivated by a deep frustration.[4] The poverty rate today is roughly the same as it was fifty years ago. How is that possible given the fact that we have learned so much in the past decade about what works to improve the lives of low-income people? Researchers at the Federal Reserve, in partnership with academics and practitioners, have been exploring myriad new interventions that cross social service silos and eschew mainstream thinking about what is transformative to combat the conditions that lead to poverty. Those ideas are captured in four books that we refer to as the What Works series on community revitalization and antipoverty work. Published by the Federal Reserve under my leadership, the What Works series brings together ideas from many sectors—community development finance, social service provision, academia, philanthropy, and others— to advance our understanding of the problem of how we create opportunity for economically disadvantaged Americans.[5]

I was surprised by how popular the What Works books would become. The Federal Reserve has printed and distributed more than 100,000 free copies (with many more eBooks downloaded and individual essays read online). It has also held over fifty conferences on these books as part of a larger "knowledge campaign"; many thousands of people participated to discuss how the themes of these books affected them in their communities across the country. Part of the books' popularity rests on the paradox I stated earlier: despite the improved capacity and knowledge on how to address poverty, we are not solving the problem. Now is the time to reflect on those insights, lift up what has worked, and imagine new business models to ensure that all Americans live lives to their fullest potential. But to be clear, this isn't about just making the existing social service systems work marginally better; this is about using our newly acquired insights to generate a breakthrough and fundamentally change our current approach to improve the lifetime opportunities of low-income people.

Building on the insights of over 250 authors in the What Works series, this book proposes the establishment of a new policy ecosystem that establishes a set of incentives to drive successful interventions in people's lives when they need it most (guardrails and airbags). I think a policy ecosystem that could do this on a mass scale must use market mechanisms to "create the vital conditions so that all people can thrive," to borrow a phrase from Tyler Norris, president of the Well Being Trust.[6] I call this set of incentives a quasi-market that values health and wellbeing, and it will rely heavily on innovations in outcomes-based financing. To be clear, these incentives are designed to improve health and wellbeing in the spirit of the World Health Organization's 1946 Constitution preamble: "a state of complete physical, mental and social well-being and not merely the absence of disease or infirmity."[7]

This new policy ecosystem would not require increases in taxes; it is about how to spend antipoverty dollars more wisely. It is also about how we can redirect some of the money we already spend on *downstream consequences* of poverty, such as poor health, to *upstream causes*, such as disinvested neighborhoods. At root, this book tackles two of the leading domestic challenges our country faces: skyrocketing medical care costs and falling economic mobility—especially for those living in poverty and communities of color struggling against generations of institutional racism. My thesis is that we can solve them both—but only by "making the problem bigger," as President Dwight Eisenhower used to counsel. We must link both problems and solve them simultaneously.

Part I: Larger Structural Issues Are Daunting, But They Are Not Destiny

There are serious structural issues facing middle- and low-income Americans. Racial inequality, the growing wealth gap, stagnant wages, and the spatial manifestations of these macro trends, such as gentrification and displacement, segregation by income and race, historical disinvestment in distressed neighborhoods, all are serious problems that need creative solutions.[8] Upward mobility was once considered a given but is now increasingly rare. For those born in 1940, 90 percent earned more than their parents; for those born in the 1980s, only half achieved that goal, according to research by Harvard University's Opportunity Insights (previously the Equality of Opportunity Project).[9] And this sense of economic insecurity is now affecting even high-wage workers. In one generation, U.S. wealth held by upper- and middle-income households (50th to 90th percentile of income earners) has fallen from 35 percent of the total to 29 percent. Most of this wealth has transferred to the top 1 percent of U.S. households, according to a study by the Federal Reserve Bank of Atlanta.[10] Many, or even most, Americans do not believe the economy works for them. In a recent CBS poll, two-thirds of Americans said the country was "on the wrong track," even though the economy had been strong and unemployment was at a fifty-year low before the pandemic of 2020.[11] The triple crises of a global pandemic, severe economic recession, and civil unrest over racial injustices make matters much worse as we reel from the calamitous events of 2020 and 2021.

Poverty in America has also become more intense in an often-overlooked development over the last fifty years. Even though the poverty rate in the United States during that time has bounced between 11 and 15 percent, it masks a much more worrisome trend—the significant growth among those who live in "deep poverty." Deep poverty refers to people who are living under half the poverty line (about $1,000 a month for a family of four). The *proportion* of people living in deep poverty has nearly doubled since the 1970s.[12] In 1976, 7.2 million were living in deep poverty, or about one quarter of the total.[13] In 2016, by contrast, the total number of people living in deep poverty was 18.5 million, which was nearly *half* of all people living in poverty.[14] These households are also more likely to be poor across generations, with children inheriting the poverty of their parents and grandparents.

I recognize that larger forces are powerful headwinds shaping the negative outcomes I have outlined thus far. In addition to the economy, so many of the systems that support us all as a society are breaking down and ossifying. Law, medicine, technology, education, and politics are also failing to promote health, wellbeing, and our humanity. This is not a book about reimagining the capitalist system or stopping those powerful headwinds. But within that context we can do much better. Other countries, with similar economic systems and facing similar headwinds, do better, and so can we. In other words, in terms of *reducing poverty*, those larger forces and trends are not destiny.

There have been many periods of severe economic and social distress like this before in American history. And they have all been followed by periods of explosive creativity, economic recovery, and civic renewal. I think we are living in one of those periods of renewal now, although it is harder to see because the creativity and rejuvenation of that renewal occur in isolated pockets around the country. When we link those places, their ideas, and promising new business models, I know we will be poised to create considerable improvements in the lives of low-income Americans, especially the nearly 37.2 million who are living in poverty.[15]

This book is based on the belief that we can do better by those low-income people and that what matters is not just the structural forces that produce these inequalities but also how we respond to them. And while this book is aimed at policymakers primarily, I hope, too, that all of us can see ourselves in a discussion of how we can create a better social safety net. In many cases that net will help catch those of us who are facing the most challenges. But it is worth remembering that we all face challenges from time to time. A better social safety net could help any one of us or someone we love. This is, in essence, a discussion of how we can all take better care of each other.

Band Aid Spending: U.S. Spending on Health Care, Social Services, and Negative Downstream Social Outcomes

Some explain our high poverty rate, and the growing number in deep poverty, by the death of the welfare state. If only we spent more on the needs of the poor, like Sweden, we would solve the problem. There is no doubt that more generous welfare spending would help greater numbers of vulnerable people get by. But the reality is that we spend a lot on the poor (more even than Sweden). Our problem is that we spend it in the wrong way and on the wrong things. And to my colleagues promoting universal basic income (UBI), I want to say that there are no shortcuts to ending poverty; it is complex and requires a delicate balance of creating opportunities in places (neighborhoods matter), ensuring an income, and other strategies that build community connections and resilience. And while an economic floor provided by a UBI could be a helpful component of a larger strategy, it is not sufficient to solve the problem.[16]

One of the important places to start this discussion is with the fact that we spend significantly more on medical care than any other country and get less for it.[17] The best overall measure for health, life expectancy, has leveled off (figure I.1) and even declined in recent years. In the 1970s, the United States was similar to other wealthy countries in terms of life expectancy and health expenditures, but by the early 1980s, something very different started to appear in the data. Now the United States is a powerful outlier. We spend significantly more on medical care and see a flattening, or even decline, in life expectancy.

The recent decline in life expectancy in the United States—from 78.7 years in 2010 to 78.6 years in 2017[18]—is remarkable given a nearly 50 percent decline in homicide rates since the 1980s,[19] alongside similar declines in smoking rates and plummeting incidence of heart disease[20] and HIV/AIDS deaths.[21] This decline in life expectancy is happening for the first time in a century (since the last global pandemic in 1918)

FIGURE I.1 Life Expectancy vs. Health Expenditure, 1970 to 2015[24]

Health financing is reported as the annual per capita health expenditure and is adjusted for inflation and price level differences between countries (measured in 2010 international dollars).

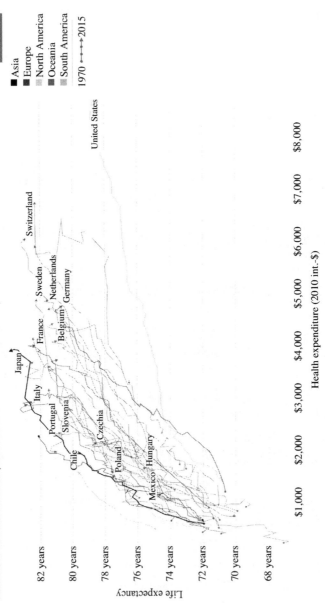

and is not the experience among any of our peer wealthy nations. Tragically, part of the answer here is increased suicide rates, but it does not explain all of what we see.[22] And, of course, COVID-19 took a heavy toll in the year from 2019 to 2020, according to Steve Woolf and his coauthors in an article in the *British Medical Journal*. Overall in that year, U.S. life expectancy decreased by one year, although the drops were significantly different for different races (0.8 years in white people, 2.7 years for Black people, and 1.9 years for Hispanic individuals).[23]

Elizabeth Bradley and Lauren Taylor made a splash in 2013 with their book, *The American Health Care Paradox: Why Spending More Is Getting Us Less*, which was built around the now-famous graph showing that the United States spends significantly more on medical care than other countries. That was a known fact. The authors added another dimension to this comparison. They provided data showing what all those same countries spent on social services—programs such as housing, nutrition, and income support programs. These and other programs are aimed at addressing what we now recognize as the *social determinants of health*, or the vital conditions for good health mentioned earlier. In that comparison, the United States is in the middle of the pack of our peer wealthy countries (figure I.2). One of the authors' theories is that our nearly inverse spending (more on medical procedures and less on social welfare) is one explanation of why our overall health outcomes are so much worse than those in other countries. As Corey Rhyan, an analyst at the Center for Sustainable Health Spending at Altarum, observed, "We spend so much on health care because we're mopping up for our lack of investment in education, housing, and other areas."[25]

Something the chart in figure I.2 does not capture, however, is the considerable amount of money that is spent on social welfare through the federal tax system. Those expenditures, by their nature, do not appear on a chart of spending. Rather, the social welfare spending captured in figure I.2 is *direct expenditures*—money paid directly by government for social services. Public resources that are financed

FIGURE I.2 Total Health and Social Service Direct Expenditures as a Percentage of GDP

Expenditures as % of GDP

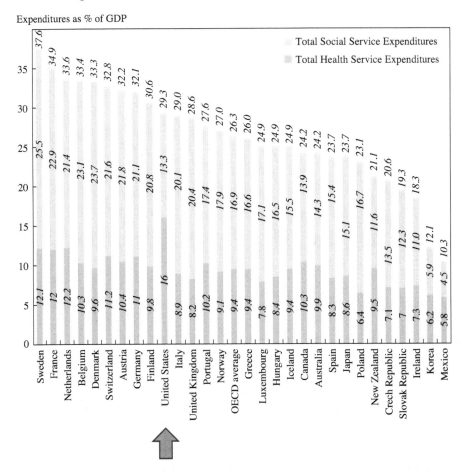

through the tax code are known as *tax expenditures*. Sometimes tax expenditures are referred to as "tax breaks with a social purpose." International comparisons look very different when these additional tax-code resources are factored in.

Christopher Howard, a political scientist at the College of William and Mary, made this observation in an important book titled *The Hidden Welfare State: Tax Expenditures and Social Policy in the United*

States. He wrote, "The hidden welfare state is almost half the size of the visible welfare state."[26] In 1995, the government spent $900 billion on the visible welfare state and $400 billion on social welfare through tax expenditures via corporate welfare, military welfare, and social welfare.[27]

The Organization for Economic Cooperation and Development (OECD) analyzes the social spending of all its member nations (essentially the world's most economically advanced countries). Every year it calculates both direct expenditures and tax expenditures used for social services. OECD calculations leave out many of the tax expenditures that Professor Howard considers "tax breaks with a social purpose," but this analysis still gives a more accurate comparison than the Bradley/Taylor figure of public resources devoted to social welfare across countries listed in figure I.2. Those calculations for 2018 are represented in figure I.3, which compares *net* social spending as a percentage of GDP at market prices in 2015. In this analysis, the United States, which was twenty-first in the OECD in terms of direct social expenditure, is second when it comes to *net* total social expenditure when tax expenditures are included (represented in figure I.3 by the diamond).[28]

Of course, total dollars going to social welfare does not measure the effectiveness of those resources. But it does make the case that the United States is not starving its social service programs. As Kimberly Morgan, in an article in *Foreign Affairs*, explains:

> In its own way, the U.S. welfare system delivers many of the same benefits as the systems in other developed countries, including health insurance, pensions, housing support, and child care. And when added together, the amount of resources the public and private sectors commit to all these forms of welfare is massive: as a percentage of GDP, for example, spending on the health and welfare of citizens is greater in the United States than in most advanced industrial economies.[30]

She argues that this spending (both direct and tax motivated), although comparable in aggregate terms, may not be as effective because it is "lopsided and incomplete."

The fact remains that we are spending more than every other country on social welfare (save for France) and still we have much worse health outcomes. Something else is going on. And the solution to that problem is not simply spending more money.

The graph in figure I.4 adds one additional crucial dimension to our understanding of the problem. It captures the mind-blowing amounts we spend on the downstream negative effects of social dysfunction in terms of costs such as incarceration, special education, enhanced policing, and lost contributions from undereducated, unhealthy, and underemployed members of our society.

The chart in figure I.4 captures in the first bar to the left what we spend on (1) medical care, (2) direct expenditures for social welfare, and (3) tax expenditures for social welfare. It also calculates the negative downstream expenditures on lost worker productivity, the criminal justice system, special education, and the costs of victimization from crime (e.g., stolen goods). All the calculations are represented as a percentage of GDP in 2019. It is staggering that we spend almost $7.6 trillion on efforts to improve the social circumstances of American citizens and on the negative social consequences of not making effective upstream investments in people.

McKinsey & Company has also attempted to quantify the cost of increased economic productivity and output if we could make the country healthier. In their report, "How Prioritizing Health Is a Prescription for US Prosperity," the authors estimate that "poor health costs the United States about 16 percent of real GDP annually from premature deaths and lost productive potential among the working-age population."[32] Primarily they looked at how improvements in population health would add to economic prosperity through "fewer premature deaths; lower rates of disability among the working population; higher labor-market participation among healthier older people,

FIGURE I.3 Direct Expenditures and Tax Expenditures for Social Welfare[29]

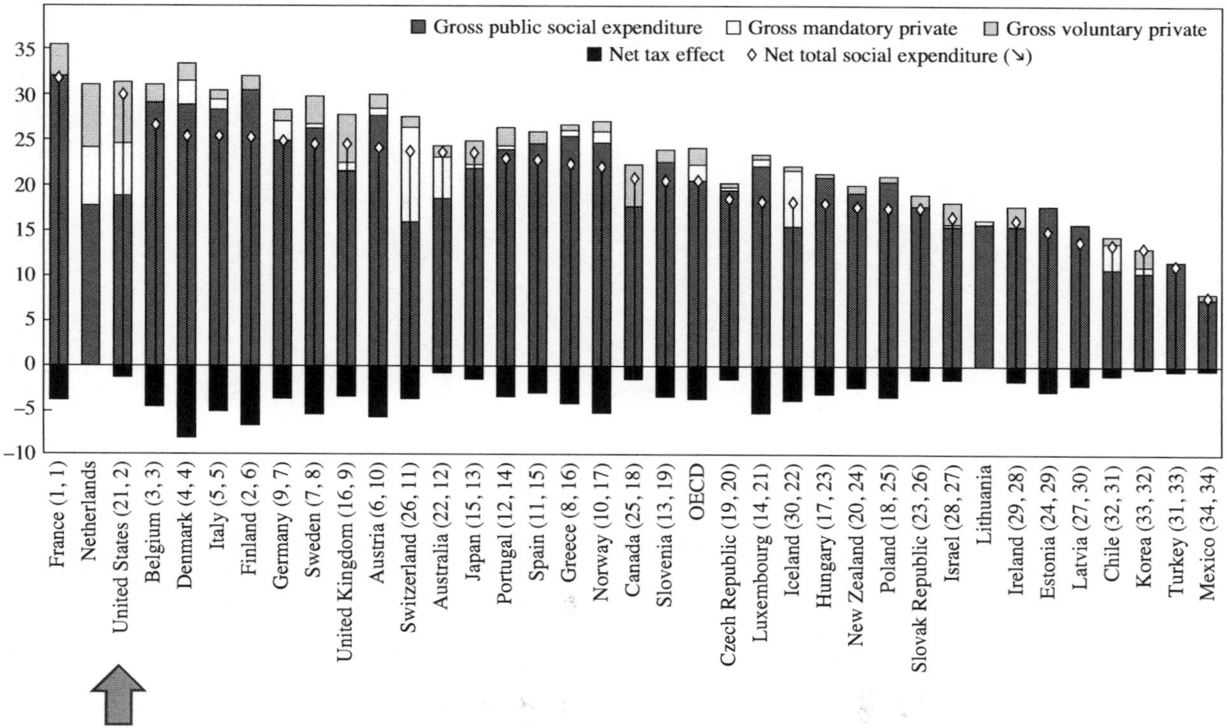

Gross public social expenditure
Gross mandatory private
Gross voluntary private
Net tax effect
Net total social expenditure (↘)
35
30
25
20
15
10
5
0
−5
−10
France (1, 1)
Netherlands
United States (21, 2)
Belgium (3, 3)
Denmark (4, 4)
Italy (5, 5)
Finland (2, 6)
Germany (9, 7)
Sweden (7, 8)
United Kingdom (16, 9)
Austria (6, 10)
Switzerland (26, 11)
Australia (22, 12)
Japan (15, 13)
Portugal (12, 14)
Spain (11, 15)
Greece (8, 16)
Norway (10, 17)
Canada (25, 18)
Slovenia (13, 19)
OECD
Czech Republic (19, 20)
Luxembourg (14, 21)
Iceland (30, 22)
Hungary (17, 23)
New Zealand (20, 24)
Poland (18, 25)
Slovak Republic (23, 26)
Israel (28, 27)
Lithuania
Ireland (29, 28)
Estonia (24, 29)
Latvia (27, 30)
Chile (32, 31)
Korea (33, 32)
Turkey (31, 33)
Mexico (34, 34)

FIGURE I.4 Social, Health, and Tax Expenditures and Negative Downstream Expenditures, by Type as a Percentage of GDP[31]

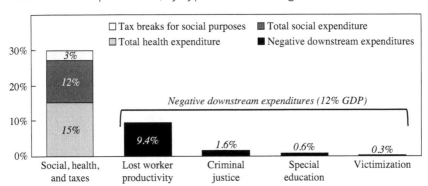

informal caregivers, and people with disabilities; and higher productivity of a healthier workforce." Improving health outcomes in five areas— "musculoskeletal disorders, mental disorders, neurological disorders, substance use disorders, and diabetes and kidney disease"—would save the economy $3.2 trillion annually.[33]

This final assessment on the cost of not making better upstream investments brings me back to my initial statement: the status quo is stupid, unfair, and expensive. We are already spending enough money to end multigenerational and deep poverty in this country. We can spend those substantial public resources more effectively and achieve better outcomes. When we tackle this problem at its roots, we will make dramatic improvements in overall health and wellbeing (using the World Health Organization definition). And as we improve those conditions to improve health, we will improve economic mobility as well. We do not lack resources; we lack imagination and the belief that we can do better.

Part II: Reasons for Optimism about the New Social Safety Net and How to Pay for It

There is a wide variation in social outcomes across the country, which suggests many of the tools and conditions to improve the life chances are local. One way to gauge this phenomenon is by measuring economic mobility. There are many ways to measure economic mobility, but a common one is with a simple ratio: the percentage of children born into the lowest quintile of parental income who land in the highest-income quintile themselves in later life.[34] The theory is that a high ratio indicates that a community has more opportunities and fewer barriers to advancement, especially for disadvantaged kids.

The United States does not compare favorably to other wealthy nations when it comes to economic mobility as it is measured in the manner explained earlier (7.5 percent). That is why the joke is that if you believe in the American Dream, you have to move to Denmark, a country with one of the world's highest economic mobility scores (11.7 percent). But the United States is a continent-sized nation with 330 million people, and the national average is often misleading because it hides significant regional variation. In fact, some parts of the country would fare quite well in international comparisons (figure I.5). The San Francisco Bay Area, for example, beats Denmark in terms of economic mobility (12.9 percent vs. 11.7 percent) and, with a population of 6 million, would be a bigger country to boot. The same is true for Boston, Salt Lake City, Seattle, and Washington, DC—all with populations close to Denmark's and with similar economic mobility scores (10.5 percent, 10.8 percent, 10.9 percent, and 11.0 percent, respectively).[35]

On the flip side of that comparison, many parts of the country are doing much worse. And it is important to keep in mind that this is despite *all* areas of the country being subject to the same federal policy and tax code, trends in technology, globalization, and other structural changes to the economy. This point deserves repeating: some areas of the United States are doing *as well as or better than* the vaunted socially democratic Nordic countries—and doing so without the much-discussed policies of Medicare for All, UBI, stronger unions, free college, and the like. At the same time that other areas—Charlotte, Atlanta, and Cleveland—are doing abysmally in terms of economic mobility within the same federal environment and similar global trends.

FIGURE 1.5 Economic Mobility across the United States

The Geography of Upward Mobility in the United States
Chances of Reaching the Top Fifth Starting from the Bottom Fifth by Metro Area

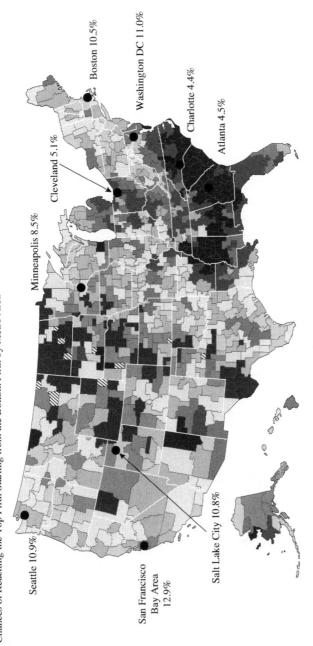

Seattle 10.9%

San Francisco
Bay Area
12.9%

Salt Lake City 10.8%

Minneapolis 8.5%

Cleveland 5.1%

Boston 10.5%

Washington DC 11.0%

Charlotte 4.4%

Atlanta 4.5%

Source: The Equality of Opportunity Project

This wild variation in economic mobility challenges the critique that if you are not tackling massive structural issues embedded in the economy, you are not tackling the root causes of poverty. What is it that is happening in the Bay Area, Boston, Salt Lake, Seattle, and Washington, DC, to allow Denmark-level economic mobility, whereas other areas, including economically prosperous places like Atlanta, Charlotte, and, to a lesser degree, Minneapolis, lag so far behind? In an effort to answer that question, Chetty and others have identified five characteristics that contribute to economic mobility. High mobility areas, according to Chetty, have (1) less residential segregation by race and class, (2) less income inequality, (3) better primary schools, (4) greater social capital, and (5) greater family stability. In other words, they have more guardrails.

Too many social reformers see as pointless any arguments that don't focus primarily on structural problems. David Callahan, in an essay in *Inside Philanthropy*, makes the case that local efforts to improve the life chances of low-income people are like growing saplings while the forest is being clear-cut. He writes, "Equity-minded foundations keep failing to zero in on the all-important sphere of political economy. Inequality mainly stems from how the U.S. economy works and, critically, the range of public policies and power arrangements that govern economic life. Yet, instead of focusing laser-like on this fundamental reality, funders embrace overly diffuse, often localized strategies that yield few larger systemic gains. They win battles here and there, while losing the war."[36]

Callahan may be right that we are losing the war, but he is essentially proposing that we build the Maginot Line (the massive French fortifications bypassed by the Nazis) and point the guns in the wrong direction. Solely focusing on macro issues is pointing the guns in the wrong direction. The Denmark-level bright spots in the United States suggest he is wrong. We have created economic opportunity in certain places around the country, which implies that we should be able to spread that success to all parts of the country. This reality also suggests that many, or even most, of the building blocks for success already exist, and they are local. That gives us more confidence that local experimentation may be the most fruitful area in which to improve the lives of the most vulnerable Americans. Federal policy should focus on how to enable these experiments to grow. As we identify and improve on the local strategies that are successful, the federal government can spread and scale these efforts so that more people benefit from them.

Twin Revolutions of Outcomes-Based Financing and Population-Health Business Models

As already shown, we spend a massive amount of money on down-stream problems (see figure I.4). Every year we spend over $3 trillion just on chronic disease (or nearly $40,000 for a family of four).[37] A significant proportion of that spending is the by-product of living under stressful and unhealthy conditions caused by poverty. "Socioeconomic status is the most powerful predictor of disease, disorder, injury and mortality we have," says Dr. Tom Boyce, chief of University of California, San Francisco's Division of Developmental Medicine.[38] In an essay in *Health Affairs* by Elizabeth Bradley and her colleagues, they summarize the extensive toll negative social determinants of health take on the nation's physical health:

> Extensive evidence demonstrates a clear relationship between a variety of social determinants and health outcomes. Poor environmental conditions, low incomes, and inadequate education have consistently been associated with poorer health in a diverse set of populations. Taken together, social, behavioral, and environmental factors are estimated to contribute to more than 70 percent of some types of cancer cases, 80 percent of cases of heart disease, and 90 percent of cases of stroke.[39]

We also spend almost half a trillion dollars yearly on efforts to alleviate the downstream effects of poverty through our direct-expenditure social welfare systems.[40] What if we found a way to spend downstream resources on upstream issues—easily more than $1.5 trillion annually—to improve people's lives so that those downstream problems—incarceration, chronic disease, poorly trained workers—never developed in the first place?

Sympathy, moral outrage, and the in-your-face suffering of downstream problems often focus us on the problems we see: the homeless person sleeping in a doorway, the chronic-disease patient using the hospital's emergency department for medical care, the low-skilled worker who needs to be retrained after losing a job. But there were many, many opportunities earlier in those people's lives when we could have intervened—with better mental health services; access to fresh, affordable food; or tutoring and mentoring to keep a struggling student on track academically. Upstream interventions like these (guardrails and airbags) could have helped put those individuals on a more viable life path and made them more resilient to the inevitable hurdles that life presents. Those upstream interventions—multiplied by the many of tens of thousands who needed them—also would have saved many billions of dollars for the systems that react to downstream social needs, such as avoidable chronic disease, incarceration, emergency medical care, among others.[41]

Bryan Stevenson, the civil rights lawyer, writes in his book *Just Mercy: A Story of Justice and Redemption* about a heart-breaking and powerful moment in the life of a condemned African American man on the day of his execution. The inmate said, "It's been so strange, Bryan. More people have asked me what they can do to help me in the last fourteen hours of my life than ever asked me in the years when I was coming up." Stevenson reflected on how this man wasn't helped when he needed it. Stevenson asks, "Where were those people when he really needed them? Where were all of those people when Herbert was three and his mother died? Where were they when he was seven and trying to recover from physical abuse? Where were they when he was a young teen struggling with drugs and alcohol? Where were they when he returned from Vietnam traumatized and disabled?"[42]

So how do we create a system that provides the proper incentives to successfully intervene in vulnerable people's lives when they need it most? How do we create a smarter social safety net that focuses on upstream needs to avoid negative downstream consequences? Is it possible to use the aforementioned $1.5 trillion to pay for a robust market that values improved wellbeing and better health? Can we create a new social safety net—one that incorporates guardrails and airbags to deliver better social outcomes with that redirected cash flow?

Part III: Plan for the Book

This book has an introduction and five chapters. This introduction summarizes key ideas and makes the case for this new approach to the social safety net. Chapter 1 reviews the history of early efforts to build a social safety net from the nineteenth century to the present. Chapter 2 focuses on what it means to have guardrails and airbags in your community. The third chapter explores how this new social safety net might work; a shorthand for this is the phrase "the market that values health."[43] To make that idea more concrete, I explore how this market might land in one place. I chose to focus chapter 4 on Hawaii because I think the state has many characteristics—not least that it is an island—that make a transition to this new approach more likely to be successful. But I think many areas around the country have similar characteristics to Hawaii and could be areas where a breakthrough is possible. And as we build, test, and improve, I think the ability to transfer this idea to bigger geographies will become more feasible. Finally, chapter 5 is a conclusion that focuses on concrete next steps to create a nationwide system of guardrails and airbags with more opportunity, wellbeing, economic prosperity, and better health for all Americans.

Chapter 1

Evolution of the Welfare State: 150 Years of Efforts to Assist Low-Income Communities and Individuals

Traditional societies relied on close-knit social ties and did not need a welfare state. Once people started living in large industrial cities in the late nineteenth century, however, a new approach to care for fellow citizens was necessary. In the United States, there have been many eras in the evolution of these welfare state efforts—from the Progressive Era, to the New Deal, to the War on Poverty.

The welfare state experiments since the 1960s have been harder to label because they have been smaller in scale and less ambitious than the earlier efforts. But they have still been significant in terms of dollars spent and insights gained. One way to describe the progression of antipoverty policy since the 1960s is a transition from a focus on "recipe thinking" to a focus on "process thinking." Recipe thinking dictated that a community needed certain "ingredients" to be successful—a clinic, a school, a grocery store, a bank, and so forth. There is no question that a community needs all these things, but as Nancy Andrews, CEO of the Low Income Investment Fund, once said, "We thought if we got the buildings right, everything else would take care of itself."[44]

Later eras, from the 1990s onward, were engaged in "comprehensive community development," recognizing that sprinkling amenities throughout a neighborhood was not enough. A better process—a plan—was needed to work across social-service sectors and build toward a shared goal. This period focused on assembling the right actors and "getting the process right." One of the more prominent examples of this approach is the "collective impact" model promoted by FSG Consulting. Collective impact relies on cross-sector/data-driven interventions with a backbone organization that shepherds the overall intervention. This approach also emphasized getting the right mix of community residents in decision-making roles so that the intervention team reflected—ethnically, culturally, and racially—the community that was being served.

This emphasis on process has resulted in some successful, comprehensive, place-based interventions, but we also know that when these interventions work, there are almost always extraordinary and rare circumstances at play. In most successful interventions, for example, there is a charismatic super-genius leading the effort who has a close friend who is a billionaire.[45] Lightning does strike, but it is hard to build a business model around that possibility. And it is impossible to replicate and scale.[46]

Today's emphasis on "process thinking" is the wrong approach. It is almost impossible to fully understand a community and its individual residents to such a degree that we can create a plan or process for improving the life chances of its residents. And as well-meaning as efforts to include all voices at a decision-making table are (or what is referred to in some interventions as a "table of tables"), it is nearly impossible to get that right too.[47] Time after time, interventions of this type simply crumble under their own weight and leave an even deeper sense of distrust in communities.

Having essential ingredients is necessary for success (ingredients matter). Having a plan that coordinates multiple sectors and actors is also necessary (process matters). Meaningful involvement from the community that allows it to have a voice in how resources are allocated and decisions are made is also necessary (community involvement matters). But something more is needed. I believe a reorientation around outcomes is critical. If we do not pay for what we want (e.g., kindergarten readiness rather than child daycare slots; high school graduation rather than remedial tutoring; permanently housed residents rather than homeless-shelter beds), then we lack the incentives to bring all the necessary elements together into one sufficient strategy to solve the problem.

Chapter 2

*Guardrails and Airbags: Better Strategies to Improve
Neighborhoods and Support Families Are the Basis for
a Smarter Social Safety Net*

Former member of the Federal Reserve Board of Governors, Betsy
Duke, wrote, "At one time, policy discussions revolved around whether
community development was about people or places. I would argue
that the debate is over and both sides won."[48] My attempt to opera-
tionalize that insight is through the concepts of "social guardrails" and
"social airbags." Guardrails are aspects of a neighborhood that guide
residents—especially children—to better outcomes by providing opportunities in education, sports and recreation, safe and affordable
housing, reasonably priced fresh food, health care, and other place-
based resources. Airbags, by contrast, are more focused on people.
Like the airbags in your car that deploy in a collision, social airbags
deploy in a moment of personal crisis.

These two ideas are a powerful way of conceptualizing what is
needed in low-income communities. They are related to other tools—
such as outcomes-based social finance—to shift our work from applying
Band-Aids to the negative downstream consequences of social problems
to tackling problems upstream, when the chances for success are best.

Robert Putnam described social airbags in his book *Our Kids* to
explain why children with resources (middle- and upper-income kids)
manage to do better than low-income children on so many outcome
measures. He refers to examples, such as the "scissor graph" (figure
I.6), that show steadily improving outcomes over time for resourced
kids on almost all social outcome measures, and stagnant or deterio-
rating outcomes for children with fewer resources.

The good news, of course, is that airbags work. The challenge is to
make sure *all* children have them and that the airbags have the appropriate predictive capabilities to deploy at the right time.

FIGURE I.6   Parental Spending on Children's "Enrichment"

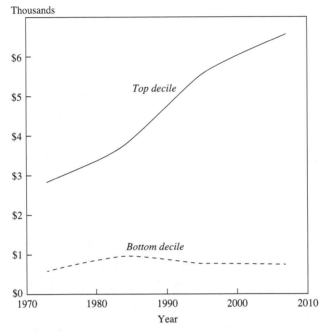

Source: Putnam (2005).

Simultaneously, however, is the need to make the community that person lives in more opportunity-rich and health promoting. These health and safety features built into neighborhoods are guardrails. While airbags deploy at critical moments in a person's life, guardrails are safety features keeping individuals from veering off into danger-ous territory. Guardrails are any community institutions, services, or characteristics that help individuals stay connected to and supported by their community. In this sense, the following serve as guardrails: schools, houses of religious worship, clubs, museums, scouts, librar-ies, Little League and other sports programs, band, drama club, dance groups, and so on. Put differently, an opportunity-rich neighborhood itself is a set of guardrails.

I recently had a conversation with a pediatrician who had a young patient struggling with weight issues. During the course of her medical exam, it became clear that this child was also suffering from depression and was contemplating suicide. The pediatrician had a hard time scheduling a psychiatrist follow-up appointment because the child was busy rehearsing for a play—by her own report, the most important and joyful part of her life. In this instance, her drama class was an important guardrail. The pediatrician felt comfortable delaying the appointment because she could see how important the play was to this young girl—keeping her from careening off the road.

When a community has multiple and overlapping supports of this type, what starts to develop is something of a "zone defense" capable of steering people clear of trouble (e.g., social isolation, risk-taking behavior) in its early stages. In that sense, the staff of the guardrail institutions—teachers, crossing guards, librarians, Sunday School teachers, music instructors, coaches, and den mothers and fathers—act as guardrails for families and kids. And that zone defense contributes to the health-promoting capability of a neighborhood.

In short, success requires listening to Betsy Duke by both helping people and improving places. But even more than that, these interventions have to be coordinated and deployed with skill so that they are appropriate over an individual's life course and the changing needs for communities. People and neighborhoods are complex organisms, and what they need changes over time. What works in one stage of life might undermine success in the next.

Coordinating both people and place-based strategies is hard. Sequencing them successfully over time is harder. But to do less guarantees failure. We have spent trillions of dollars executing strategies (e.g., job training or drug treatment) and place strategies (e.g., affordable housing or Opportunity Zones) on disconnected and uncoordinated people over the past fifty years and have almost no examples that show those interventions substantially changed lives or communities. In medicine, success over disease requires correct treatment that gets the dose, intensity, and duration right. We need a smarter social safety net that successfully invests in people (airbags) and places (guardrails) so that we get the treatment right over time.

Chapter 3

Financing Guardrails and Airbags: Creating a Market That Values Health

Any market has *consumers/buyers* and *producers/sellers*, in addition to the *connectors*, who facilitate transactions.[49] Markets are dynamic, changing in response to new information, new players, and innovations. In this case, we are talking about a market that is meant to improve wellbeing, especially for vulnerable populations. For this market to work, *sellers* must create value by improving wellbeing for vulnerable people. *Buyers* are willing to pay for more wellbeing and health. Buyers are diverse and include health insurers, health care systems, the federal government, employers, cities/counties/states, and others who benefit from a healthier, happier, and potentially more productive population. And *connectors* will provide the mechanisms and vehicles to connect the *buyers* and *sellers*; they are the sinews of this market.

Buyers of Health

There are a number of entities that are interested in paying for better health outcomes. Some of them are obvious: the federal government, through its Medicare, Medicaid, and Veterans Administration health programs, is the 800-pound gorilla in this category. State governments are also in this bucket. Maryland, for example, has been exploring an alternative payment model for its rural hospitals using a capitated payment model, "where providers are paid for serving a defined population instead of being paid more for doing more."[50] Massachusetts was a leader in this approach to paying for medical care, which is often referred to as "global budgeting." Oregon is experimenting with coordinated care organizations that do something similar. North Carolina is developing an aggressive statewide plan to address the upstream social determinants of health. And other states are experimenting with a wide variety of Medicaid waivers for further experiments in using medical dollars to pay for improving the social determinants of health, such as affordable housing.

Other buyers of health include health insurance companies, big employers (especially those who self-insure their employees), hospital systems that are concerned about the costs associated with readmitting patients without the ability to bill for additional procedures, and foundations that care about health (e.g., Robert Wood Johnson, Kresge, and health conversion foundations, such as the Colorado Health Foundation, the Well Being Trust, and the California Endowment). And, of course, as we get more comfortable with the expanded concept of health as wellbeing, there are many other funders who pay for the building blocks for good health: affordable housing (Department of Housing and Urban Development and the Low-Income Housing Tax Credit), jobs (Small Business Administration and the New Markets Tax Credit Program), transportation (infrastructure spending), and good schools (Department of Education and state governments). Impact investors are described as investors who want to "marry money to meaning." As the market that values health develops, they might become a more significant buyer of health as it becomes clearer that upstream investments in the social determinants of health can accomplish many of their social improvement goals as well as improving health.

Producers/Sellers of Health

The second actor in this market is what I call the *producer* of health, which essentially is any person or entity that promotes wellbeing. Education is a driver of better health outcomes; therefore, teachers and schools are producers of health. Children who attended a high-quality preschool in the first five years of their lives—which helps build the foundation for school success, including reading—enjoy better physical health in their midthirties, including lower blood pressure and less obesity.[51] Income is a driver of health. Therefore, anyone who provides a living-wage job is a producer of health. There are many other factors that help kids succeed, and one proven example is having an engaged adult outside your immediate family who cares about you. A study following generations of children growing up in Kauai found that "at-risk" children with a nonparent caretaker, such as an aunt, a teacher, or a coach, were much more likely to thrive later in life.[52] Therefore, high-quality youth mentoring is a producer of health. The list here could go on, but in the end, anyone who helps low-income people or other at-risk communities take control over their own lives, or anyone who helps impart a feeling of agency and an opportunity to gain control over one's destiny, is a producer of health.

When resources from the buyer category of this market start to flow, my belief is that it will activate those producers of health just mentioned. But I think the creative power of this marketplace will help surface new types of producers of health that may not spring to mind. One type of producer of health with transformative potential is artists. Artists, almost by definition, not only see the world as it is, but imagine how the world could be. And through multiple media, they communicate those ideas to a wider audience. The artist/community entrepreneur could be a key player in helping a vulnerable community to thoroughly examine the trauma it has endured and imagine a future with more hope and agency, which will translate into better wellbeing and health. The artist/community entrepreneurs could also help communicate that vision through the community in a way that generates buy-in and momentum for positive change.

Connectors

The third category of actors in the market that values health comprises those who connect the buyers of health to the producers of health. These *connectors* are often Pay for Success strategies and vehicles, such as the Kresge Foundation's Strong Families Fund or the Equity-with-a-Twist tool developed by the Low Income Investment

Fund.[53] The Healthy Neighborhood Equity Fund (HNEF) is a connector. Maggie Super Church, a cofounder of HNEF, was motivated by a simple question: "Why can we invest in a company that makes a pill that lowers blood pressure but we can't invest in a neighborhood that does the same thing?"[54] Her fund has an interesting mix of buyers who are investing in neighborhoods to make them more salutogenic: banks, hospitals, and insurance companies, in addition to many government entities and philanthropies.

Pay for Success strategies are connectors. Perhaps the most famous Pay for Success tool is the social impact bond. To date, this tool has been narrowly applied to interventions that have elements of a randomized controlled trial. But that is not an essential feature of this tool, and I can see it applied in a broader way. Imagine being an investor in the Ready-to-Learn-at-Kindergarten Bond that supports the producers of health in early childhood in your community. And technology may play a bigger role in this connecting process. Neighborly.com was an online municipal bond platform that could create customizable bonds of this type to support the funding of early childhood enrichment. Neighborly could also have developed connector tools to support other salutogenic investments in schools, parks, broadband internet connection, and micro electrical grids for nonpolluting renewable energy.

Of course, the best possible connector is a health entity that is either an organization that is both an insurance company and a medical care provider (e.g., Kaiser Permanente or Intermountain Healthcare) or an insurer that owns the majority or all of the downstream medical-care cost risk for a population that is relatively contained (e.g., a large, self-insured corporation or a rural county with one health insurer). These entities would be on the vanguard of the population-health business model, where they are paid per person / per year to keep people healthy. Unlike the largely fee-for-service medical system, their business incentives are aligned with health (in the World Health Organization sense) rather than treating illness. The healthier their members, policyholders, employees, or residents, the better off they are financially. That arrangement is the ultimate connector, since it provides significant motivation to work upstream to improve the vital conditions to improve health, which creates downstream medical-care cost savings. That insurer/medical care provider, leading a coalition of other buyers of health, would create pockets where a market that valued health could grow.

Chapter 4

Hawaii Case Study: How an Island State Can Point the Way

Chapter 4 is a thought experiment to explore how this new approach lands in a particular place. To be clear, this market that promotes wellbeing and health is simply a tool. It works only if the people and communities in a place are interested and willing to use it. And, of course, as a tool, it serves the needs and wants of the people who will use it for their benefit. The tool does not create value; the community does.

I chose to focus on Hawaii in this chapter because it possesses a number of attributes and characteristics that make success for this approach more likely. But there are many other communities around the country—and the world, for that matter—where a number of characteristics align to create favorable chances for a breakthrough to achieve this new business model.

The challenges in Hawaii are similar to those in other parts of the country. Although it is a stunningly beautiful place, the economy had been based on plantation agriculture. Many of the laborers who migrated to Hawaii from around the world (Japan, Philippines, Portugal, etc.) were low income. And the transportation revolution that brought the islands competition from around the world for its commodity agricultural goods, also brought tourists. While the shift from an agricultural to a tourism-based economy created many jobs, they are not high paying. And living in Hawaii is expensive, which is why a third of the state's population that is living above the poverty line is still Asset Limited, Income Constrained, Employed (ALICE), according to a study by the United Way of Hawaii.[55]

Perhaps the most striking aspect of the Hawaii example, however, is that the downstream medical-care cost risk is concentrated in just a few actors. Two large health insurers (Hawaii Medical Service Association [the Blue Cross/Blue Shield provider] and Kaiser Permanente), along with state and federal Medicaid and Medicare programs, have the lion's share of downstream medical-care cost risk. (And a high percentage of those in the Medicare system are Medicare Advantage policyholders, which allows greater flexibility than Medicare alone.) These four buyers of health (along with other smaller health insurers, like UnitedHealthcare and Wellcare; big employers, like the U.S. military; and large hotel and tourist businesses) could coordinate to make upstream investment in the social determinants of health in a way that could produce downstream savings for all involved.

Hawaii also has many producers of health, especially its numerous high-quality community-based social-service organizations. Housing and education are essential contributors to wellbeing and health, and Hawaii is unusual—and fortunate—to have only a single school district and one housing authority for the entire state. Both are committed to the goal of improving health.

And it is important to note that despite the appearance of many villages and towns, each island is a county and has only a single local government. Each island has one mayor. This dramatically limits the number of bureaucratic entities, compared with other places (e.g., 108 separate member governments make up San Francisco's Association of Bay Area Governments).

Hawaii is home to some of the most forward-thinking Federally Qualified Health Centers in the country. The Waianae Coast Comprehensive Health Center and Kōkua Kalihi Valley Comprehensive Family Services both provide topnotch medical care *and* have adopted their whole neighborhoods as "patients." They both are engaged in a number of efforts to enhance the social and economic conditions that lead to improved health. And increasingly, hospitals are being paid an up-front capitated amount to keep patients healthy, which incentivizes the hospitals to find ways to reduce avoidable visits and medical treatments.[56]

There are many connectors in Hawaii. The state has many vibrant, locally rooted banks, many wealthy charitable foundations, and a small but growing number of community development financial institutions. And assistance from groups based in the continental United States, such as the Local Initiatives Support Corporation (LISC), could increase the capacity in this category. LISC, for example, has been developing a Hawaii Opportunity Fund. This fund could be a power-ful *connector* tool to allow hospitals, banks, and others to coinvest in the social determinants of health.

Overall, Hawaii has the right mix of *buyers*, *producers*, and *connectors* to make a market that values health work. And on top of these advantages, Hawaii has a built-in, high-quality pre- and post-evaluation of any systemic intervention to improve the conditions that improve health. Most of the relevant data for such a study are aggregated administratively at an island level because each island is a county. And, because the state is made up of islands, there is less seeking of care and resources outside administrative boundaries than occurs in the continental United States. Of course, lessons learned in Hawaii would be studied with an eye to sharing those insights to other island-like communities in other parts of the United States.

Chapter 5

Conclusion and Next Steps

The final chapter focuses on concrete next steps for building a nation-wide version of this new approach to the social safety net. Chapter 5 will also discuss the new public policies, business practices, and investment strategies that will help spread guardrails and airbags and scale them.

CHAPTER 1

Evolution of the Welfare State

150 Years of Efforts to Assist
Low-Income Communities
and Individuals

CREATING SOCIAL WELFARE SYSTEMS THAT CARE for those who are struggling is a relatively recent phenomenon. Over the past 150 years in the United States, there have been many different approaches to helping people adapt to the challenges and disruptions associated with the modern economy and urban life. At root, these efforts were designed to improve opportunities to live healthy and productive lives. This chapter sketches out how some of those programs have evolved over the years and lands us at today's debate over how we should organize our social services sector and provide communities with more opportunities.

Part I: Efforts to Establish an American Welfare State

This chapter is presented in three parts. First is a brief overview of social welfare strategies over the late nineteenth and twentieth centuries in the United States. Part 2 concentrates on one new strategy that grew out of the War on Poverty—community development. And part 3 focuses on the place-based initiatives of the twentieth and early twenty-first centuries that focused on improving neighborhoods (places) as a way to help people escape poverty.

The history is not a particularly positive one. Even though a far lower percentage of Americans are living in poverty today than 150 years ago, too many individuals and families are suffering and not living to their fullest potential. It is both a moral issue and an economic one. The status quo is expensive in terms of paying for the negative effects of failure in the social sector (e.g., incarceration, chronic disease, underemployment, and remedial education). And weak links in that system make us all more vulnerable to health and economic threats as we learned in the COVID-19 outbreak that began in 2020. In a pandemic, no one is safe unless we are all safe. That is a good lesson for social welfare too.

Caring for Low-Income Communities in the Nineteenth and Early Twentieth Centuries in the United States

Historians bristle when people say that the Civil War (1861–1865) was a battle between the "Industrial North" and the "Agricultural South." The North did have more factories than the South, but to say it was an industrial economy is wrong. Almost half of workers in the North had ties to agriculture (compared with 2 percent today), and although the percentage was higher (80 percent) in the South, both societies were overwhelmingly agricultural.[1] In 1860, with only one in five Americans living in a city (defined as 2,500 or more inhabitants), the country was overwhelmingly rural.[2]

Americans, attracted by factory jobs and growing urban economies, did not start moving into cities in big numbers until the 1880s. This shift in our society set three powerful trends in motion:

1. Competition for industrial jobs drove down wages in many industries.
2. Competition for places to live near those jobs drove up rents.
3. Leaving home for the city cut social ties that were traditionally provided by families and small, tight-knit communities.

A significant result of these three trends was the creation of slums or ghettos, where struggling low-income Americans concentrated. For some, the distance traveled from farms to ghettos was short, whereas others crossed oceans and continents. Many of the new arrivals thrived, but for those who did not there was not much of a social safety net. Churches and charities provided some relief, as did local governments, but these efforts were small in comparison with the growing need for support.

There were many waves of this phenomenon: Southern and Eastern Europeans in the late 1800s and early 1900s; poor Southern whites and Blacks during the Great Migration to Northern cities starting after 1915; dramatic increases in immigration from Asia and Latin America after 1965; and, of course, it continues today in many cities worldwide as rural populations flock to cities seeking opportunity. The United States became a majority-urban nation by 1920,[3] and the worldwide population reached majority-urban status in 2008.[4]

There were early coordinated efforts to care for and help stabilize new arrivals to the cities. Pioneers, such as Jane Addams in the late 1800s and early 1900s, addressed these issues through the Settlement House movement, which had almost five hundred campuses nationwide by 1920 (considered the first place-based/cross-sector intervention for low-income communities).[5] And tight-knit immigrant communities were able to provide for many of the needs of new arrivals. These efforts, however, were small and local.

With the arrival of the Great Depression in the 1930s, local interventions were no longer a match for that era's mass unemployment and

FIGURE 1.1 "The White Angel Bread Line" by Dorothea Lange, San Francisco, California, 1933[9]

mass misery. By that time, American society was urban and industrial, and downturns in the economy were more than a "cold shower," in the economist Joseph Schumpeter's famous phrase; they were moments of widespread suffering and political instability. In 1933, the gross national product had dropped in half from the 1929 level, and one in four workers was without a job.[6] Relief systems for the poor were beyond their breaking points, as dramatized by the ubiquitous sight of breadlines in American cities (see figure 1.1). As Franklin Roosevelt said in his second inaugural address, "I see one-third of the nation ill-housed, ill-clad, and ill-nourished."[7] During the New Deal, the federal government had two choices, according to Chicago mayor Anton Cermak in his congressional testimony: It could send relief to Chicago; if not, it would have to send troops.[8]

The economic development and jobs programs of the New Deal—and later, the massive spending to mobilize for the Second World War—got the country working again. After the war, a combination of successful public policies and economic growth drastically reduced the percentage of Americans living in poverty. Between the 1940s and the early 1970s, the U.S. poverty rate was estimated to drop from 33 percent to a low of 11 percent in 1973.[10] In real terms, family income grew almost 75 percent from the end of WWII to the mid-1960s.[11] In the fifty years since then, however, the poverty rate has been stubbornly persistent between 11 and 15 percent (figure 1.2). Meanwhile, the absolute number of Americans living in poverty has risen with the nation's population growth. The Supplemental Poverty Measure, which the U.S. Census has used since 2011, is more accurate since it factors in government income supports, among other adjustments.[12] Interestingly, it has tracked the historical official poverty measure from the War on Poverty relatively closely.

Experiments in the 1960s: The War on Poverty

Even in the midst of the postwar economic boom, it was clear that poverty still had a grip on American life. Writers like Michael Harrington, in his book *The Other America* (1962), put a spotlight on lingering urban and rural poverty in the United States. Thanks to powerful allies (e.g., organized labor and the Civil Rights Movement), the federal government launched an effort to eradicate poverty in 1964. President Johnson announced that his administration had "declared a war on poverty in all its forms, in all its causes, and we intend to drive it underground and win that war."[13]

The historian James Patterson observed that President "Johnson, [Sargent] Shriver, and the others who developed the war on poverty . . . were not radicals. They were optimists who reflected the confidence of contemporary American liberal thought." According to Patterson, "They were not so much concerned about inequality. They focused

FIGURE 1.2 Poverty Rate and Number in Poverty: 1959 to 2020

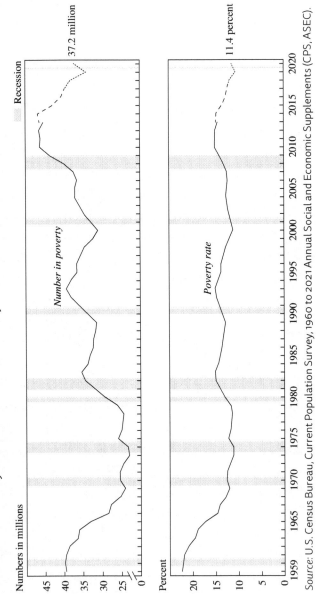

Recession

Numbers in millions

37.2 million

Number in poverty

Percent

Poverty rate

11.4 percent

Source: U.S. Census Bureau, Current Population Survey, 1960 to 2021 Annual Social and Economic Supplements (CPS, ASEC).

instead on programs to promote greater opportunity—a politically attractive goal."[14]

True to that vision, the War on Poverty would not be a radical program of income redistribution. The programs would focus on creating opportunity. The lead agency for the War on Poverty was the Office of Economic Opportunity, which was responsible for multiple programs in health, employment, education, and housing.[15] There were efforts to eliminate hunger through the Food Stamp Program, reduce education disparities through Head Start and additional funding through the Elementary and Secondary Education Act, provide access to legal advice (Neighborhood Legal Services), and create opportunities to participate in improving communities as a volunteer (VISTA) and as a community member (Community Action).[16] New health centers would be built (federally qualified health centers) to provide medical care and also adopt the whole neighborhood as the "patient" in keeping with the community-oriented primary care philosophy.[17] The Department of Housing and Urban Development (HUD) was created in 1965, and in the words of its first secretary, Robert Weaver, to an assembly of U.S. mayors, "We are involved in the exciting and creative business of bringing all our resources and energies to bear in solving the problems of your cities."[18] And the Social Security Amendments of 1965 created the state-run medical insurance programs for the elderly (Medicare) and the poor (Medicaid).[19]

Part II: Experiments in the War on Poverty to Create Quasi-Markets to Improve Low-Income Neighborhoods

One important legacy from the War on Poverty in the 1960s is "community development," an approach to revitalizing low-income areas that grew out of the Ford Foundation's Gray Areas program.[20] The idea was to fund local nonprofit corporations that were rooted in and rooting for struggling communities. It was an attempt, according to

Robert F. Kennedy, to not treat single issues contributing to poverty, but to "grab the web [of urban poverty] whole."[21]

These community development corporations (CDCs) got their start with the Bedford Stuyvesant Restoration Corporation in New York City in the mid-1960s. CDCs were nonprofit but subject to market discipline in their pursuit of better local social outcomes and a stronger local economy. "These groups were born of the activist spirit of the '60s—products of the War on Poverty and the civil rights movement, and reactions to the negative effects of the federal urban renewal program," according to housing scholar Avis Vidal, who noted that "these groups often began as community service or community action agencies and later moved into community economic development."[22] Today, there are over four thousand CDCs working in communities in all fifty states.[23]

CDCs and social service providers were often constrained by lack of capital, and their projects and initiatives often required extra help to underwrite financially. Loans, initially from the pension dollars of nuns and churches, were the first into this financial breach. Those loans spawned a new type of institution to meet the credit needs of low-income neighborhoods, the community loan fund. The loan funds were the precursors to community development financial institutions (CDFIs) that received substantial federal funding beginning in the 1990s.[24]

CDFIs were partners to the creative new transactions that were financing the revitalization of communities around the country; they took more risks, and their patient capital often brought about the innovative transactions that harmonized multiple sources of capital (private, public, and philanthropic). Over time, these transactions became more routine, and more likely to be funded by traditional banks. Today, there are over a thousand CDFIs certified by the U.S. Treasury[25] with over $35 billion in assets.[26] CDFIs come in many forms (loan funds, credit unions, banks, etc.), but are uniform in that they "are profitable but not profit-maximizing," according to their umbrella association, the Opportunity Finance Network. "They put community first, not the shareholder."[27]

The government funding programs that grew this small network of CDCs and CDFIs came from federal block grants (Community Development Block Grants and HOME Investment Partnership for affordable housing) and tax incentives in the form of investment tax credits (the Low Income Housing Tax Credit and the New Markets Tax Credit). There were private-sector sources of funding as well. Many banks were motivated to engage CDCs and CDFIs as a way to meet their requirements under the Community Reinvestment Act (CRA) of 1977. The CRA was an explicit policy to end "redlining," a practice where banks would take deposits from a community but not lend back to it because it was low-income and considered to be too risky. This practice stripped wealth out of communities and was particularly devastating to low-income African American neighborhoods.

Philanthropy also played an important part in building this new system. In addition to the work of the Ford Foundation mentioned earlier, many leading philanthropies invested in the creation and growth of the community development network. This extended beyond grant making as well; many foundations experimented with new ways to finance community development work through program-related investments (PRIs), which provided a below-market rate of return for their investment in return for funding activities that promoted the foundations' missions. Another development was mission-related investments (MRIs), which were similar in promoting a positive social outcome but with a market-rate return. PRIs and MRIs provided an early model for the subsequent impact investing movement.

This new network of players, funded by public and private sources, created something that operated like a market. It was not a market in the simplest sense, but it was fostered by many government subsidies and regulations that boosted the "demand" side of the equation. This government-supported quasi-market had many advantages over the older, top-down, Washington-based approach to community revitalization. Different local players would come together to develop a particular property or project. They could then disassemble and recombine with new partners for new projects, providing greater flexibility and nimbleness as times and needs changed.[28]

The glue keeping these different groups working together was the funding from the many sources of community development finance, government at all levels, foundations, and banks. This funding provided the effective "demand" that created a market for community revitalization. CDCs and CDFIs were the first into this marketplace, but other for-profit real estate developers and banks followed. In the end, this network of public and private players was successful in creating tens of billions of dollars of investments into low-income neighborhoods annually.

Overwhelmingly, these investments were in real estate. In the early years, most of the investing was in affordable housing (often with social services for residents). Later, however, there was more investment in health clinics, charter schools, homeless shelters, and grocery stores in food deserts. There were practical reasons for this; lending against property is easier for banks since there is collateral against the loan. But the theory behind the community development strategy was that if you could improve the physical place—the disinvested neighborhood—then you would create new opportunities for the people who lived there. This was the "recipe" thinking referred to in the introduction. To paraphrase Nancy Andrews, former CEO of the Low Income Investment Fund, getting the right mix of buildings in the neighborhood is not enough to put a community on the path to prosperity.[29] The challenge of creating opportunity in low-income communities proved to be harder than the "recipe" theory of change predicted.

Access to Capital Was Not Enough to Power Low-Income Communities Out of Poverty

Many in the antipoverty/social justice movement, such as Gail Cincotta and others, believed that a significant barrier to the progress out of poverty was the lack of access to the financial products and services that would help build wealth. It was the driving force for policies such as the Community Reinvestment Act and the creation of community development financial institutions and later funding programs, such as the New Markets Tax Credit, which funded "near bankable" deals (especially small businesses).

The Community Reinvestment Act, mentioned earlier, was one policy response to that problem. The law was intended to undo the nearly thirty years of formal federal policy and private sector practices that discouraged lending into low-income neighborhoods as a strategy to reduce risk of financial loss to both government (through its guarantee and insurance programs) and the private sector. This practice was especially damaging to the local economies of African American neighborhoods and to the efforts at creating wealth for individuals and families living there. In essence, it set the racist practices of limited bank lending to nonwhite borrowers in concrete for the next forty years, as figure 1.3 shows the access to credit for areas such as Beverly Hills but the lack of it for East and South Central Los Angeles.

The wealthier neighborhoods in northern Los Angeles County (e.g., Beverly Hills) and along the coast (e.g., Santa Monica) got the best ratings, while neighborhoods to the east and south, such as El Monte and Compton had worse ratings in terms of risk.[30]

In its simplest explanation, CRA is a requirement for banks to make loans and investments back into the communities where they take deposits. There is no target on how much this should be; the banks are asked to meet the credit needs of the low- and moderate-income people in a manner that is "safe and sound" in the language of the law.[31] The scale of their investment is hard to gauge, but an estimate

FIGURE 1.3 1939 Home Ownership Loan Corporation map of Los Angeles.

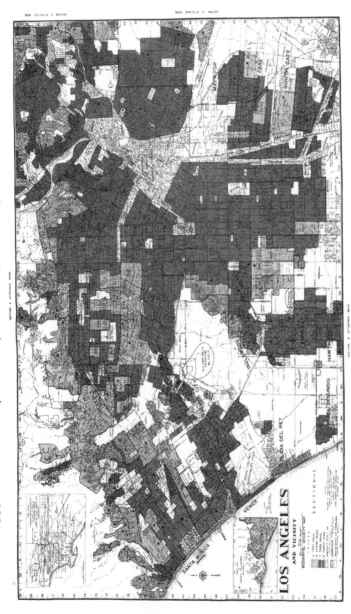

The wealthier neighborhoods in northern Los Angeles County (e.g., Beverly Hills) and along the coast (e.g., Santa Monica) got the best ratings, while neighborhoods to the east and south, such as El Monte and Compton had worse ratings in terms of risk.

from the Urban Institute puts the annual amount invested in low- and moderate-income communities to meet CRA obligations over $400 billion in 2018 alone.[32]

But early in the community development movement, certain leaders questioned the value of capital access without other reforms and policies. Paul Lingenfelter of the MacArthur Foundation, for example, questioned this assumption in a closing keynote address to a meeting in Durham, North Carolina, in 1994. It was an early meeting of what we now refer to as the CDFI industry. The speech, titled "Half Truth," posited that access to capital was only one of many barriers that low-income people experienced.

"Community development financial institutions in the United States have been built on a half-truth. The half-truth is: Lack of access to capital is a primary factor in perpetuating, if not causing, poverty. The capital gap is an important problem and providing access to capital will alleviate poverty and improve the quality of life for the poor." Lingenfelter went on to say, "Why is this only half true? We all know that capital must be combined with other things in order to sustain itself or grow. Without certain essential partners, capital will not grow, it will dissipate."[33] The intervention in low-income areas that Lingenfelter sought was one that used capital as a tool to unleash the energy and creativity of residents, but it combined that tool with other interventions to create a thriving place.

Over the years there have been many other efforts to increase the flow of capital into low- and moderate-income communities to produce more affordable housing and community facilities, and to help families stabilize their finances and build assets, to start businesses, and build schools, clinics, and stores. They include many programs already mentioned (Community Development Block Grants, HOME Investment Partnership Block Grants, and investment tax credits—New Markets and Low-Income Housing Tax Credits), and many other programs that amounted to tens of billions of dollars annually from the Small Business Administration; U.S. Department of Agriculture; older

HUD programs, such as Urban Development Action Grants and Section 8 vouchers; and newer tax incentives, such as Opportunity Zones. In all, trillions of dollars have flowed into low-income communities, but those resources did not trigger the hoped-for positive feedback loop of economic growth and wealth creation. It helped many, for sure, and had there been more resources, perhaps even more people would have benefited. But with all that investment, you would think we would have at least a handful of examples where capital flowing to community development and other community-based organizations would have triggered a neighborhood renaissance. We simply don't have those examples. Access to capital to finance community resources (clinics, affordable housing, grocery stores, and schools) may be necessary, but it is not sufficient to create thriving, opportunity-rich communities.

Part III: "Place-Based" Interventions—Coordinating Cross-Sector Efforts to Help Neighborhoods Thrive

As mentioned earlier, the Settlement Houses of the nineteenth century may have been the first cross-sector/place-based interventions to improve the life chances of low-income Americans, but this strategy was attempted many more times throughout the twentieth century. Perhaps the most well-known example came in the 1960s with the Model Cities efforts that were part of the War on Poverty. Model Cities required comprehensive strategies and significant and meaningful resident participation. Overall funding was significant, but the requirement to cover an ever-growing list of sites (150 by the end) stretched the program too thin. That effort, however, achieved little and lost political support; it was ended in 1974 by folding that and other War on Poverty funding into the Community Development Block Grant program.[34]

Many younger readers familiar with thriving urban areas will find it hard to believe how place-based efforts like Model Cities and the Gray Areas program struggled against the declining fortunes of cities in the late 1960s and 1970s. New York City was famously on the brink of bankruptcy in 1975. And many now-booming cities, such as Atlanta, Boston, and Chicago, lost more than 10 percent of their populations.[35] According to Federal Reserve economist Jordan Rappaport, "Nearly half of large cities shrank by at least 10 percent. St. Louis, Cleveland, Buffalo, and Detroit each shrank by more than 20 percent. Vast stretches of urban land were left virtually deserted."[36] As late as the early 1980s, Brookings researchers concluded that "continuing population declines in most large U.S. cities seem irreversible."[37] Turning around a struggling neighborhood is hard; doing that in a city that is dying is nearly impossible. The shift in attitudes and desire to be back in cities was a boost for the community development sector, although it brought new challenges in the form of gentrification and displacement of low-income residents.

Place-Based Efforts in the 1990s

After the failure of Model Cities, cross-sector/place-based efforts fell out of favor in the 1970s and 1980s, but they experienced a resurgence in the 1990s. New residents and new investments flowed back into cities. And for the neighborhoods that were bypassed in this renewal, community development and community development finance marshaled capital from multiple sources to invest and provide a range of services and interventions in an effort to turn those neighborhoods into places of opportunity. This approach usually involved a range of players, including health, education, economic development, job training, affordable housing, and more.

There were a number of promising place-based efforts in the early 1990s sponsored by both philanthropy and government. One effort that had both Republican and Democratic support was the Empowerment Zones (EZ) program during the Clinton administration. In their book on this program, *Collaborative Governance for Urban Revitalization*, Michael Rich and Robert Stoker put it this way:

Republicans lauded the virtues of free markets and maintained that government was the problem; the most effective way to promote prosperity in distressed inner-city neighborhoods was to get government out of the way by removing regulatory barriers, reducing or eliminating taxes, and fostering entrepreneurism. Democrats, on the other hand, favored continued support of a variety of federal grant-in-aid programs that provided cities with resources for affordable housing, economic development, public safety, job training, education, and services for low-income children and families. EZ designees, for the first time, got both.[38]

EZ cities were required to create a vision for improvement in partnership with local stakeholders and to improve conditions by coordinating interventions from multiple social service sectors with every effort to "reduce red tape." The plans were required to have performance benchmarks and sought to connect the neighborhood to opportunities in the region. The original EZ program targeted sites in six cities: Atlanta, Baltimore, Chicago, Detroit, New York, and Philadelphia-Camden. Each site received a $100 million grant, and access to federal tax incentives, private facility bonds, and waivers of regulatory hurdles. The areas of focus typically had poverty rates that were twice as high as the city as a whole.[39]

Only Baltimore and Philadelphia-Camden got positive results, even though they were the two poorest cities in the group. "Our point is not that the social and economic context is irrelevant," Rich and Stoker observed, "our point is that poor local governance can squander a favorable context and good local governance can overcome a difficult context."[40] Rich and Stoker concluded that success rested on local leadership—inside local government and among a wider network of actors including business and philanthropy. It is hard to assess the long-term benefit of the EZ program, but thirty years later, Philadelphia-Camden and Baltimore seem to have had difficulty sustaining their earlier successes.

Another important cross-sector/place-based intervention in the 1990s and 2000s was the HOPE VI program that was started in the George H. W. Bush administration to replace existing distressed public housing—the heavily subsidized affordable housing stock more commonly referred to as "the projects." Launched in 1992, it evolved under the Clinton administration to be a more ambitious attempt to create vibrant mixed-income and mixed-use neighborhoods in the places that had been neglected for so many years. The program spent $5 billion to replace "severely distressed public housing projects." Of the 1.3 million apartments in the public housing portfolio, the National Commission on Severely Distressed Public Housing determined that 86,000 were severely distressed.[41]

A 2004 assessment of the program by the Urban Institute, *A Decade of HOPE VI: Research Findings and Policy Challenges*, concluded that the program had many successes, including the demolition of uninhabitable housing. "In many cities, HOPE VI has replaced these distressed developments with new, high-quality housing and has spurred important innovations in design, management, and financing. For the first time, the federal government has implemented a mixed-income model at a meaningful scale—combining deeply subsidized rental housing with other affordable units and even market-rate housing."[42] The report also listed some shortcomings of the program, including (1) many residents who received housing vouchers were unable to find better housing in opportunity-rich neighborhoods, (2) fewer new homes were built than destroyed resulting in a net loss of affordable homes, and (3) many residents did not fare well with the relocation process and lost their social networks of support.

The federal government was not the only one betting on place-based interventions in the 1990s and early 2000s. Between 1990 and 2010, foundations invested over $1 billion according to Anne Kubisch in *Voices from the Field III*.[43] Those foundations included some of the leading philanthropies in the United States, such as Annie E. Casey, The

California Endowment, Edna McConnell Clark, Enterprise, Hewlett, MacArthur, Pew Charitable Trusts, Robert Wood Johnson, Rockefeller, and Surdna.

Kubisch and her coauthors assessed forty-three major comprehensive community initiatives (including government efforts) for the Aspen Institute's Roundtable on Community Change.[44] These place-based interventions embraced a comprehensive strategy to invest in services for the residents, improvements to the physical place, and development of the local economy. There were many positive developments for individuals that resulted from these efforts but "few, if any, were able to demonstrate widespread changes in child and family well-being or reductions in the neighborhood poverty rate."[45]

Kubisch and coauthors praised these forty-three interventions for using "systems thinking" to tackle multiple challenges simultaneously. The problem, in terms of implementation, was that it required "capacity that under-resourced organizations in distressed neighborhoods often do not have." Successfully executing a community change effort "requires managing a complex web of relationships among residents, funders, intermediaries, neighborhood organizations, public sector agencies, private sector financial institutions, and consultants," according to Kubisch. Keeping all those players aligned and incentivized is tricky and can be derailed by "the lack of real or perceived self-interest; cultural, historical, racial, or legal barriers; or the direct personal and institutional costs associated with making the relationships successful."[46]

The evaluators concluded that working through those many complex and complicated relationships did leave the communities with more capacity than they had before. And that capacity, combined with a renewed respect for the value of learning in real time and making adjustments to strategy along the way, was an important legacy of the forty-three place-based efforts. It also inspired another round of efforts at place-based interventions during the Obama administration.

The Obama administration attempted to incorporate learnings from Enterprise Zones, HOPE VI, and the forty-three examples already mentioned into their place-based interventions, Choice Neighborhoods, Promise Neighborhoods, Sustainable Communities, and Strong Cities/Strong Communities (SC2), among others. The new administration arrived with ideas and optimism. The new HUD secretary had input from over a hundred experts who gathered their suggestions in a book-length report titled, *Retooling HUD for a Catalytic Federal Government: A Report to Secretary Shaun Donovan.*[47]

These were ambitious programs that intended to bring in all the best learnings on how cross-sector and place-based interventions could work. They were new, too, in their deliberate effort to get government out of its silos and the agencies working together to create opportunities across domains (education, jobs, housing, etc.) as a strategy to improve life chances in a neighborhood. These multiple programs were overseen by a team in the White House known as the White House Neighborhood Revitalization Initiative. And these efforts were all heavily influenced by the approach known as Collective Impact, promoted by FSG Consulting, which was popular at the time.[48]

The HUD-led Choice Neighborhoods may have been the most ambitious of those place-based efforts to revitalize a struggling neighborhood. In the foreword to an Urban Institute and MDRC (a nonprofit originally known as Manpower Demonstration Research Corporation) report assessing the early progress of the program, Assistant HUD Secretary Katherine O'Regan wrote, "Choice intends to help communities address long-term neighborhood disinvestment comprehensively, through connected strategies to rebuild housing, offer supportive services to housing residents, create quality educational and economic opportunities in the surrounding neighborhood, and improve public safety."[49] She went on to observe that this initiative was "the Obama Administration's locally driven, place-based approach to addressing entrenched poverty and inequality in communities."[50]

The initiative was divided into three domains—housing, people, and neighborhood. On the housing front, HUD would replace the substandard existing public housing that concentrated low-income residents with a mix of high-quality and energy-efficient housing that was aimed at serving both low-income subsidized tenants and middle-income tenants paying market rents. HUD would coordinate people-oriented services to improve health, safety, employment, and education of the families and individuals in the target development and surrounding neighborhood. Finally, the focus on neighborhood was intended to create opportunity through improved schools, public assets, public transportation, and access to jobs.[51] "Building on lessons from HOPE VI and other place-based initiatives, Choice has the potential to accelerate the development of revitalized, mixed-income neighborhoods," according to O'Regan.[52]

Again, however, the ambition of this program—its grasp—was not achievable given its capabilities—its reach. The innovations in thinking and tactics were many and mutually reinforcing: "Choice's ability to leverage new and improved social services, infrastructure, and private-sector development in the neighborhood; sustain a mixed-income population; improve local schools; and change local policies to promote coordinated community improvement efforts."[53] But as in so many prior efforts, the complexity of the strategy stymied success.

There is a question as to whether the resources for this program ever matched the grand vision, which is a familiar complaint for every anti-poverty program ever attempted in the United States. There were certainly positive transformations of the housing stock, as was the case with HOPE VI. But a report by the International City/County Management Association concluded that over three years of the program, in the three cities where they focused their research, the Choice Neighborhoods interventions experienced "very little tangible improvement other than vague references to greater awareness of the community's needs."[54]

Another place-based program, Promise Neighborhoods, also struggled. It was a program modeled on the Harlem Children's Zone and aimed "to improve educational and developmental outcomes for students in some of the country's most distressed urban, rural, and tribal neighborhoods by aligning a suite of cradle-to-career services in a designated geographic footprint," according to a Government Accountability Office report.[55] Barack Obama, as a presidential candidate, believed this could be a cornerstone in his administration's effort to reduce poverty. During the campaign, he said, "The philosophy behind the project is simple—if poverty is a disease that infects an entire community in the form of unemployment and violence; failing schools and broken homes, then we can't just treat those symptoms in isolation. We have to heal that entire community. And we have to focus on what actually works."[56] (One hears the echoes of Robert Kennedy's call to "grab the web whole.") As Obama's call to action outlines, the program was a place-based effort that expanded the focus from just a low-performing school to a broader intervention recognizing that the community has a significant influence on a child's education.[57]

Like all the place-based programs, Promise Neighborhoods put an emphasis on community input and decision making. "Community engagement is crucial to the program," according to an analysis from the Urban Institute. "Promise Neighborhoods aim to center community voice at every step, not only creating new services and improving connections to existing ones but also ensuring the kids and parents they're serving have input in where investments are made."[58] Incorporating that input, along with the unique challenges and assets that exist in all places, would allow for maximum customization of the program. "Place-based initiatives provide communities the flexibility to address their unique needs and interrelated problems by taking into account the unique circumstances, challenges, and resources in that particular geographic area," according to an Urban Institute report.[59]

The program has continued for the past decade; it was folded into the Every Student Succeeds Act. And although the Trump administration threatened to cut funding to the program, the outlays for it increased slightly through 2020.[60] Since its inception, the federal government has awarded $430 million in grants to seventeen cities.[61]

There have been challenges with this program too, in part because of its design—funding is only three to five years (although the goal is to create a supportive "cradle to career" pipeline of services, which is clearly a longer-term initiative). The focus over the entire period of childhood (eighteen-plus years) also creates challenges based on coordinating across so many organizations serving different ages in the life cycle. Finally, there is a problem over time with residents moving in and out of the neighborhood where the intervention is concentrated. That intervention is less likely to work if people are coming and going.[62]

The place-based program with some of the most promising results is an older HUD program known as Jobs Plus. It was piloted first in the mid-1990s with the intent of creating a better approach to helping public housing residents get jobs that helped them advance themselves and their families. The model had some early successes in boosting the annual earnings of participants. It was expanded to more sites and got a big boost in 2015, when HUD granted $24 million to nine public housing authorities.[63] Since 2015, HUD has awarded $63 million to twenty-four public housing agencies.[64]

In 2015, HUD joined with MDRC to engage in evaluation of the effort with help from the Center for Urban and Regional Studies at the University of North Carolina at Chapel Hill and the National Initiative on Mixed-Income Communities at Case Western Reserve University. The initial report states that "Jobs Plus is a place-based program that is rooted and operationalized in a specific locale, to serve the needs of that particular population. The program is designed to help people living in public housing increase their levels of employment and earnings. At its core, Jobs Plus is structured around three mutually reinforcing parts, all of which focus on improving residents' employment, earnings, and well-being."[65]

The three parts—employment, earnings, and well-being—were designed to provide public housing residents with the support, training, and connections to find better-paying work and if they had good jobs, to keep them. Employment-related services included things like help with job searches, coaching, training, and other support services, such as childcare. The earnings component focused on the idea to "Make Work Pay," which, among other things, did not penalize participants who started earning more by increasing their rent under the standard public housing formulas. Finally, well-being strategies included efforts to create stronger social networks within the community. Tangible examples of this included carpooling to work and providing some childcare coverage for each other during job shifts.

The relatively narrow focus of Jobs Plus and the willingness to address the "benefits cliff" that is often a disincentive to earning more has made this program a success. But in general, we know relatively little about the effectiveness of the many Obama administration place-based programs. And while many of these programs were either operated with reduced funding or were eliminated by the Trump administration, Choice Neighborhoods and Promise Neighborhoods continue into the Biden administration's tenure.

Other Recent Place-Based Initiatives

The Living Cities collaboration announced an $80 million investment into the "Integration Initiative" in 2010 to "create game-changing innovations that address the intractable problems affecting low-income people."[66] The initiative focused on five cities—Baltimore, Cleveland, Detroit, Newark, and Minneapolis/St. Paul—with the intent to "create a new framework for solving complex problems; challenge obsolete conventional wisdom; and drive the markets to work on behalf of low-income people." Does any of this sound familiar? There was a phase two of the effort launched in 2014.

Living Cities embraced the FSG Consulting Collective Impact model and used creative financing to build their cross-sector/place-based interventions. They provided $3 million in grants; another

$4 million in below-market, program-related investments from participating foundations; and $15 million in loans, according to a 2019 summary analysis report by RTI International, an independent nonprofit research institute.[67] And also keeping with the themes from the many other similar efforts already listed, the end result was not what one would have predicted given the goals and the initial plan. The report authors interviewed multiple participants in the program and came to this conclusion: "Constantly changing implementation strategies and tools, lack of clear communication, and staffing turnover led to increased site uncertainty and disrupted implementation, hindering sites' effectiveness." Again, too many moving parts, evolving goals, and communication challenges overwhelmed the effort.

Other place-based efforts continue to limp along. They include the Strong, Prosperous, and Resilient Communities Challenge (known as SPARCC), funded by the Robert Wood Johnson and Ford Foundations; an effort by the California Endowment in fourteen low-income communities known as Build Healthy Communities Initiative; and a city-led effort in San Francisco, known as HOPE SF, that tries to take the best of the HOPE VI program, incorporating more tenant-friendly elements, such as not displacing any residents.[68] Again, after years of planning, organizing, and investing, these efforts have often improved the physical environment with new housing and other amenities, but there is still no evidence that they dramatically improved the lives of the low-income residents.

However, we are certainly learning through all these scores of place-based efforts. There are many other specific place-based efforts that could be recounted in this section. An excellent overview of them can be found in an Urban Institute summary, "Tackling Persistent Poverty in Distressed Urban Neighborhoods: History, Principles and Strategies for Philanthropic Investments."[69] But time after time the assessments of these interventions seem to arrive at similar conclusions. The place-based intervention was too brief, or too uncoordinated, to turn a low-opportunity neighborhood into a high-opportunity one. Or the assessment is that neighborhood interventions are unable to do that without taking many other (maybe impossibly too many) considerations into account, as James M. Ferris and Elwood Hopkins conclude in their thorough 2015 study of place-based interventions. "Although for some funders place-based initiatives will make the most sense as an investment of time and resources, they can no longer be viewed as isolated efforts, de-coupled from public policy and market forces," write Ferris and Hopkins. "The linkage of neighborhoods to larger systems, such as metros and regions, and the recognition of the impact of market forces and public policy on efforts to address spatially concentrated poverty cannot be ignored."[70]

Most now agree with sentiment articulated by Meir Rinde in a 2021 *Shelterforce* article:

> While their methods and specific goals varied, the CCIs [Comprehensive Community Initiatives] all sought to bring focused resources and the lessons of past revitalization initiatives to poor, urban neighborhoods in order to effect broad change at the individual, neighborhood, and systems levels. They aimed to help local groups organize their communities, develop leaders, improve the physical infrastructure, boost their economies, enhance access to human services, and strengthen social bonds. But like the Ford Foundation's initiative, the efforts largely failed to make a lasting measurable impact.[71]

Too often, we are learning what doesn't work, but that is not the whole story. In all these interventions we see increased capacity to execute on an intervention. And there is much greater sensitivity to incorporating resident input. "Nothing for us without us" is now the mantra that all place-based interventions embrace. And finding new ways to bring community voice to the conversation is an area that is showing great promise.

One example of this, in my opinion, is embodied in the work of Rebuild Metro, a neighborhood improvement nonprofit in Baltimore. Rebuild Metro is taking a quarterback role in building a coalition of community leaders, faith-based institutions, community-based organizations, and businesses to revitalize the Johnston Square neighborhood "to become a safe, walkable neighborhood complete with diverse housing choices for all people and anchored by thriving businesses, supportive services and institutions," in the words of their vision statement. The organization calls for the following:

> Sustaining and vibrant neighborhoods provide equitable residential development, housing choices and are supported by businesses to cater to their daily needs. A mixed income and diverse housing stock can support people of different economic backgrounds and lifestyles simultaneously as well as give people a chance to stay local even as their needs change over time by creating and preserving a range of affordability options and housing types. A diverse retail corridor creates business synergies, supports daily needs and creates opportunities for social experiences.[72]

This effort is both bottom up (community led) and closely coordinated with top-down power from the city and other local institutions. Paul Brophy, a community development pioneer and adviser to the group, says, "The City has provided substantial financing assistance, public improvements, and decisions about what to demolish, what to rehab, and where new homes and businesses can locate. A cooperative police department is working to make the neighborhood safer."

Brophy concludes, "Slowly but surely, these neighborhoods are getting stronger, climbing up from the bottom of neighborhoods in Baltimore, seeking to compete more successfully for businesses and residents. Sometimes getting the neighborhood to a new normal requires a decade or more, illustrating that improving distressed areas is a marathon not a sprint." And all the while, Rebuild Metro is walking a fine line "between failing because the neighborhood brand is so weak that houses can't be sold, and lighting a market fire and causing prices to go too far up."

One other place-based intervention with some success is the Purpose Built Communities network. Purpose Built has been successful in improving communities by clearly defining the neighborhood where they intervene and pursuing strategies around three themes: (1) mixed-income housing, (2) cradle to career education pipeline, and (3) community wellness (not just medical care but a focus on the social determinants of health). Perhaps the secret ingredient in the success of this cross-sector/place-based intervention is the role of the "community quarterback." Each Purpose Built Community has an independent nonprofit organization whose sole purpose is organizing the community revitalization project among the many participants. The community quarterback "aligns partners and resources from all sectors—including neighborhood residents—and sets strategy for the overall effort based on the community's vision," according to the Purpose Built website.[73] Purpose Built provides its consulting services to sites at no charge, thanks to philanthropic support.

The conditions in neighborhoods of concentrated poverty were created over decades—arguably centuries—and the solutions must be long term and reflect the complexity of the challenge. The Purpose Built Communities network has started to yield positive, and in some cases, dramatic results. In both the East Lake neighborhood of Atlanta and the Bayou District in New Orleans, construction of new mixed-income housing, early learning centers, and other critical neighborhood infrastructure, both built and civic, have decreased crime to levels well below their city's averages and increased student achievement in elementary all the way through high school and beyond, in the case of East Lake.[74] They are prime examples of how a neighborhood-based approach can change the life trajectories of residents, especially Black residents and other residents of color, experiencing deep poverty by making long-term, holistic, cross-sectoral investments.

Conclusion: How Can We Build on the Experiments of the Last 150 Years?

It has been a long road from the Settlement Houses in the 1890s to HOPE SF and Promise Neighborhoods today. The next-generation efforts to battle poverty must build on the lessons of the past 150 years. Lessons like the need to harmonize multiple sources of capital (public, private, and philanthropic); how to coordinate multiple interventions simultaneously in a place-based way; how to provide tools to the community so that its members can co-create their own solutions; and how to create capacity at the local level to execute these interventions and adjust them as they learn by doing, and finally understanding that these interventions take time—this is a marathon and not a sprint as Paul Brophy counsels.

But given all this learning, we still must recognize that place-based efforts that follow many of the foregoing principles still struggle. One explanation, according to Patrick Sharkey, is that any local intervention must contend with the rising or falling fortunes of the region. He writes in *Stuck in Place: Urban Neighborhoods and the End of Progress toward Racial Equality*, "Policy experiments from the past several decades have made clear that place-based programs, by themselves, are likely to be overwhelmed by broader forces affecting the fortunes of entire segments of the urban populace, entire cities, and entire metropolitan areas."[75]

And yet, focusing on a region- or metrowide strategy leaves struggling neighborhoods ill equipped to take advantage of good times (e.g., strong economic growth) or weather bad times. "Even in times of urban growth, disadvantaged communities and specific segments of urban populations have been left behind, and these same communities are hit hardest in times of downturn," according to Sharkey.[76]

So what are the other necessary elements to a strategy that can improve the opportunities in a place, and connect the people to those opportunities without displacing them? One answer is to reimagine the marriage of people and place-based strategies. A key additional element to add to any intervention is to build on the community development finance model that focused on real estate—a strategy to improve a place. The examples that have been provided here demonstrate that a thriving community needs more than buildings. They also demonstrate that a community needs more than just access to capital. To create a thriving community requires physical as well as human capital solutions. What we need is to combine the existing tools of community development that created a quasi-market to improve the real estate in neighborhoods (place-based) with a new type of quasi-market for human capital development (people-based).

Paul Grogan, president of the Boston Foundation and one of the founders of the Local Initiatives Support Corporation, tackled this question in the *Investing in What Works for America's Communities* book in 2012. In looking to the future of community development, he wrote, "What then is the future of community development? It lies in turning the architecture of community development to meet urgent challenges of human development. How to turn a successful community organizing and real estate development system toward the goal of increasing educational outcomes, employment success, family asset building, individual and community resilience to weather setbacks? As an industry, we need new strategies to face these challenges."[77]

That is, basically, what this book is arguing for—a quasi-market that improves neighborhoods and communities while it simultaneously improves the life chances of individuals in those communities. This more vigorous, better-funded, and better-coordinated approach marries both place and people strategies in a market that values health and wellbeing. That is the subject of chapter 2.

CHAPTER 2

Guardrails and Airbags

Better Strategies to Improve Neighborhoods
and Support Families Are the Basis
for a Smarter Social Safety Net

YOUR ZIP CODE IS MORE IMPORTANT than your genetic code for predicting your health. This shocking observation was highlighted in the report from the Robert Wood Johnson Foundation's Commission to Build a Healthier America in 2014.[1] The infographic in figure 2.1 is from that commission; it shows that life expectancy near Washington, D.C., Metro stations vary from a high of eighty-four years in Montgomery County to a low of seventy-seven years in the central city. The reason for this is very simple: your body is the sum record of your challenges and opportunities. And "too many neighborhoods have too few opportunities and too many challenges," according to Dr. Doug Jutte in *Pediatrics*.[2] In the final analysis, health happens in neighborhoods. Those added challenges and too-few opportunities in zip codes translate into worse health and earlier death.

This chapter explores how we can engineer more health-promoting (i.e., salutogenic) neighborhoods with opportunities for education, housing, transit, work, and stronger social and community bonds.[4] These elements of a salutogenic neighborhood are what I refer to as guardrails. But guardrails only get us so far.

FIGURE 2.1   Variation of Life Expectancy in Washington, DC, by Metro Stations[3]

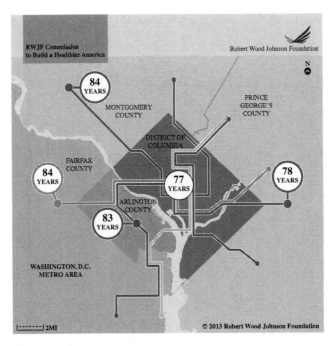

A companion concept that helps create more opportunities for success in life—and better health—is "social airbags." As mentioned in the introduction, this idea of social airbags comes from Robert Putnam, who coined the term in his book *Our Kids*. Airbags are interventions at critical moments in someone's life that either help to mitigate the damage from a bad circumstance or nudge someone in a direction that potentially leads to a better outcome.

An airbag in a car has sophisticated sensors that detect a collision immediately and deploy at the right time and with enough force to shield the passenger from harm. Similarly, a social airbag would have sensors and predictive capabilities to anticipate needs and deploy at the right time. An example might be tutoring in response to falling grades in school or family and child counseling as a response to divorce.

Together, guardrails and airbags could ensure that people don't fall through the cracks—especially kids.

Social Determinants of Health

The social determinants of health are the foundational concepts to making a market that values health. The understanding that social support and community ties influence your health is an old idea—ancient Greek and Chinese texts referenced it—that has only recently been gaining traction outside medical and public health circles, thanks in part to the work of the Robert Wood Johnson Foundation.[5] But as far back as 1948, the World Health Organization defined health as "a state of complete physical, mental, and social well-being and not merely the absence of disease or infirmity."[6]

For too many years, the focus on what explained good health rested on three pillars: (1) good genes, (2) good medical care, and (3) good behavior. All three, however, have proven deficiencies for explaining good health outcomes. Gene expression, for example, is shaped and influenced by the environment. The study of epigenetics reveals that a stressful environment (e.g., crime-plagued neighborhood) can "turn on" certain health-harming genes. Good medical care is important, but it turns out that your health is influenced far more by circumstances outside your doctor's office. Michael McGinnis's research, which has been replicated many times, shows that inadequate medical care explains only a small fraction (maybe up to 20 percent) of premature deaths.[7] Moreover, even countries that have access to universal high-quality medical care still have dramatic disparities in health outcomes. The groundbreaking 1980 Black Report in Britain, for example, found that the death rate for unskilled workers was twice the rate as that for professionals even though both groups had access to great and free medical care.[8] The subsequent Acheson Report (1998) had similar findings.[9] And behavior, the third pillar, is also important to good health, but it is almost impossible to influence. Almost all efforts to change behavior around diet and exercise fail. A possible exception may exist around smoking, but that was the result of a pattern of changes in law, culture, architecture, and policies that made it harder to smoke.[10]

Research from scientists at the University of California, San Francisco, medical school, for example, demonstrated that ongoing stress affects the length of telomeres, which, like the bit of plastic at the end of a shoelace, effectively cap and protect the ends of the chromosomes that contain your DNA. More stress is equated to a shorter cap.[11] This shorter cap length is tied to the aging process. The evidence is clear: living in a stressful environment results in shorter telomeres and more advanced aging, which is why we have lines like the one in Tracy Chapman's song "Fast Car": "His body's too young to look like his."

There is also a large body of research that demonstrates the strenuous effort your body exerts to return to a state of normalcy after stressful circumstances. Scientists refer to this normal balance as homeostasis, and the effort (and cost) to your body to achieve and maintain that state is called allostatic load. We can measure allostatic load with a simple cheek swab and get immediate evidence of how hard someone's body is struggling with their surroundings and circumstances. It will not come as a surprise that allostatic load is much higher in communities of color and low-income communities.[12] And high allostatic load is associated with flooding the body with stress-response hormones that contribute to inflammation, premature aging, and earlier death.[13]

There is something protective about your social circumstances, which helps answer a question posed by Harvard epidemiologist Nancy Krieger: "Why is it that not all people exposed to germs become infected and not all infected people develop disease?"[14] One of the pioneers in social epidemiology, John Cassel, attempted to answer that question in his famous essay, "The Contribution of the Social Environment to Host Resistance." In it, he argues that we are constantly being bombarded by pathogenic agents and yet we have predictable patterns of infection and disease that disproportionately affect socially vulnerable people. He writes, "The question facing epidemiological inquiry then is, are there categories or classes of environmental factors that are capable of changing human resistance in important ways and making subsets of the people more or less susceptible to these ubiquitous agents in our environment?"[15]

The things that make someone more susceptible to those "ubiquitous agents" are strongly associated with a lack of status, social connections, and support. It is part of why better health outcomes are associated with things like better education and higher income. A college graduate will live, on average, nearly a decade longer than a high school dropout.[16] Kids in poor families are more than four times as likely to be in less than "very good" health compared to kids in the highest-income families.[17] Health issues like chronic disease, obesity, violence, and other ailments melt away as people overcome the layered consequences of living in poverty.

Control of Destiny Brings Better Health

Berkeley professor S. Leonard Syme has a theory that the most important driver of improved health is control of one's destiny. "It has been known for centuries that people in the lowest social classes have the highest morbidity and mortality rates. What is not known is the reason for this phenomenon," writes Syme.[18] What is it about being poor that harms health? Is it substandard housing? Lack of access to medical care? Of course, all these issues are linked (and with many others that I could have listed). But it is very hard to isolate and study them in a way to try to identify the causal relationships between certain aspects of being poor and poor health.

A breakthrough, however, in our understanding of how control of destiny might be the driver of health came with the research of Michael Marmot in his paradigm-shifting "Whitehall" study in 1978, in which he analyzed the health outcomes for 18,000 British civil servants.[19] All the subjects were employed. All had access to free, high-quality medical care. And none were poor. And yet there were dramatic differences in life expectancy across every step in job ranking from the lowest—cleaning staff, guards, and the like—to the highest administrative class, effectively the chief executives. Strikingly, the second-highest class, physicians, lawyers, and other professionals, still had nearly double the rates of disease and early death as the highest rank. This pattern was repeated in the step down to the clerical class and again to the lowest rank, designated as "other" (figure 2.2). This insight was a huge shock. It was well known that impoverished people lived shorter lives with the presumption that deprivation—such as lack of shelter or good nutrition—drove those differences. But this study overturned that understanding because all the subjects were steadily employed government workers, living in an advanced society (the London metro area) with full access to high-quality, free, universal medical care. And yet, there was a fourfold difference in mortality rates across the study population.

Most people also believed the common phrase of the time, "don't work so hard, you'll give yourself a heart attack." But, instead, what the Whitehall study paradoxically found was that the people with the least authority and responsibility were the ones who were most likely to die of a heart attack.

Figure 2.2 reports age-adjusted all-cause mortality rate ratios by employment grade, for three periods of follow-up. A mortality rate ratio reports the proportion of deaths in a given group divided by the proportion of deaths in the reference group. There are four grades in the British Civil Service employment hierarchy: administrative (highest), professional/executive, clerical, and other (lowest). The professional/executive grade has been used as the reference group, so its mortality rate ratio is 1.0 by definition.

What seemed to distinguish the lives of people at different ranks in the civil service was the degrees of control they had over their cir-

FIGURE 2.2 Social Gradient in Total Mortality, Whitehall 25-Year Follow-up[20]

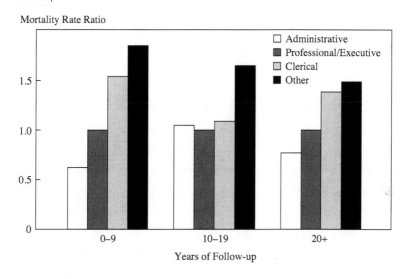

Mortality Rate Ratio

Legend:
☐ Administrative
▨ Professional/Executive
▨ Clerical
■ Other

Years of Follow-up

cumstances and destiny. Being the boss can be stressful, but one chooses that stress. And the boss is usually in a position to take a day off with a sick child or buy a new furnace when the old one breaks. In other words, the boss has some level of control over unexpected setbacks. A sense of control, status, and satisfaction in work add up to something even more: hope.

"Hope is the key to having a good biological system and a good future," according to Syme. "Hope means having a community you can have pride in."[21] Creating an ecosystem of interventions that provide hope for every American is not a pie-in-the-sky dream; it is a very achievable way to improve the health of the nation and generate economic savings. And one sure-fire way to engender hope is to create neighborhoods that promote health and wellbeing (guardrails) with individual supports that promote good risk-taking, dreaming of dreams, and staying out of trouble (airbags). The task before us is to find ways to pay for these health-improving interventions by redirecting resources to population health business models and Pay for Success financing.

Guardrails in Neighborhoods Powerfully Influence Health

Life expectancy varies dramatically by neighborhood because where you live—a place with too few opportunities and too many challenges—can damage your health. Our understanding of how these negative effects harm health is backed by mountains of research that span decades. Margery Austin Turner and Ruth Gourevitch summarize extensive research on four mechanisms that harm the long-term life-chances of neighborhood residents: "the availability and quality of services, crime and violence, the role of peer groups and social networks, and access to employment opportunities."[22]

A breakthrough study with proof of causation of how neighborhoods influence life outcomes came from Harvard researchers Raj Chetty and Nathaniel Hendren in their study "The Impacts of Neighborhoods on Intergenerational Mobility: Childhood Exposure Effects." In that study, they followed 7 million children from birth to adulthood and found measurably better outcomes for every year spent in a more opportunity-rich neighborhood: "The outcomes of children whose families move to a better neighborhood—as measured by the outcomes of children already living there—improve linearly in proportion to the amount of time they spend growing up in that area, at a rate of approximately 4% per year of exposure." They also found increasingly worse outcome for every year spent in a low-opportunity neighborhood.[23]

Amy Edmonds, Paula Braveman, Elaine Arkin, and Doug Jutte[24] succinctly summarize the insights of this large and growing body of scholarship in the following paragraph:

Poorer neighborhoods generally have more crime, pollution, fast-food outlets, and ads promoting tobacco and alcohol use[25] and often lack safe places to play and exercise.[26] Residents of high-poverty neighborhoods are more likely to live in substandard housing that can expose children to multiple health hazards including lead poisoning and asthma.[27] Perhaps less obvious but equally important is the fact that children living in poor neighborhoods are more likely to attend underperforming schools[28] and have fewer job opportunities[29] which can limit social mobility[30]—and therefore health across generations.[31]

And all the negative effects can add up to something even more damaging than each individual harm. So many challenges, with little ability to mitigate or avoid them, can contribute to a very serious "toxic stress" and do tremendous harm (especially in children), according to Dr. Jack Shonkoff and his colleagues at the Harvard Center on the Developing Child.[32] Toxic stress experienced over long periods of time is a disaster for health and literally damages your body at the molecular level. Many expensive adult illnesses have their roots in adverse conditions in childhood, according to a recent National Scientific Council on the Developing Child working paper. "Three chronic health impairments in the United States—cardiovascular disease, diabetes, and depression—together account for more than $600 billion in direct health care expenditures annually (above and beyond their indirect costs, such as lost productivity)."[33]

On the flip side, it is not hard to imagine a neighborhood that has all the elements—the guardrails—that can promote health and well-being. This is because most neighborhoods have them. These guardrails tend to fall into three main categories: (1) institutions and activities that promote a sense of connection to a larger community (volunteer associations, clubs, sports leagues, religious institutions, art and artists), (2) guardrails that help meet our more practical needs of jobs, food, shelter, and safety (employers paying a living wage, supermarkets with affordable high-quality food, affordable and safe housing, community policing and other emergency services that reduce the threat of violence while simultaneously building community), and finally, (3) institutions that feed our need to learn, develop job skills, and grow intellectually (high-performing schools, community colleges, museums, and well-funded libraries). These are all valuable services and institutions in their own right, but together they do something really special; they provide the overlapping support and engagement—a nurturing ecosystem—to help all residents reach their potential. This is the "zone defense" I mentioned in the introduction.

There is not enough research on how an improved neighborhood with more guardrails might reduce stress and build a sense of hope in residents. Several large research projects are underway, including one by the nonprofit MDRC on the Purpose Built interventions across the country.[34] The evidence base for the health-improving aspects of these types of interventions will likely follow the example of a 2021 study published in the *American Journal of Preventive Medicine*. "Despite the growing recognition of the importance of neighborhood conditions for cardiometabolic health, causal relationships have been difficult to establish owing to a reliance on cross-sectional designs and selection bias," according to the authors. "This is the first natural experiment to examine the impact of neighborhood revitalization on cardiometabolic outcomes in residents from two predominantly African American neighborhoods, one of which has experienced significant revitalization (intervention), whereas the other has not (comparison)." The results were improved cholesterol profile and improved blood pressure.[35]

To make this concept of neighborhoods that are either health promoting or harming more concrete, Dolores Acevedo-Garcia, professor of human development and social policy at Brandeis University, draws a powerful contrast between two typical neighborhoods (using data from actual neighborhoods only three miles apart in a U.S. city). She compares Neighborhood A, a high-opportunity community, with Neighborhood B, a low-opportunity community, in a recent report from the surgeon general (excerpted in the box that follows).[36]

Not surprisingly, there is a very troubling racial inequity aspect to neighborhoods like the two just described here. Acevedo-Garcia has determined that there are nearly 10 million children living in places like Neighborhood B in her assessment of the 100-largest U.S. metropolitan areas. Most of the children who live in these neighbor-

A Tale of Two Real Communities Less Than 3 Miles Apart (Representative of Myriad Similar Communities across the United States)

Neighborhood A (high opportunity) With two high-quality early childhood education centers nearby, children in Neighborhood A get a jump-start on the education ladder. Nearly two-thirds of 3- to 4-year-olds attend preschool. Math proficiency is almost universal (95 percent) among fourth graders. Four of every five adults 25 years of age and older have a college degree. A community rich in highly educated adults may increase expectations among children for their own education and work prospects and may positively influence their attitudes and actions about college attendance.

With so many highly educated adults, the neighborhood's unemployment rate in 2019 (3.8%) is less than half that of the entire metropolitan area (9.8%). The poverty rate (9.6%) falls considerably below the average (17.1%) for the metropolitan area.

The neighborhood also hosts a variety of healthy resources. For example, several parks and green spaces offer areas in which children can engage in physical activities, which may reduce the chances of obesity and associated health problems. Most of the neighborhood's food establishments are considered healthy food retailers, which increases access to proper nutrition. Health care facilities are plentiful and close by. In fact, 178 health care facilities are located within 2 miles of Neighborhood A, making it closer in proximity to health care resources than 94 percent of all neighborhoods in the metropolitan area. This proximity to health care providers likely reduces travel times for people seeking health care, which in turn yields greater utilization of routine health care services and lower utilization of emergency room care.

Neighborhood B (low opportunity) Children in Neighborhood B face a host of obstacles to opportunities and wellbeing. Only 9 percent of 3- to 4-year-olds attend preschool, and not one high-quality early childhood education center is nearby. By fourth grade, almost two-thirds of students are not proficient in math, limiting their future math

(Continued)

A Tale of Two Real Communities (continued)

achievement and their subsequent college attendance and labor wages. Among adults 25 years of age and older, only one in five have earned a college degree.

Low levels of education are accompanied by high levels of unemployment and poverty. One-third of adults are unemployed, which may affect youths' expectations of their own employment prospects and result in weaker networks of employed adults who can help young people find jobs. Nearly 60 percent of residents live below the poverty line, and 92 percent of students are eligible for free or reduced-price lunch at school. Such concentrated poverty in neighborhoods and schools is associated with poor physical and mental health, as well as low student graduation rates and future earnings.

The physical conditions and resources in Neighborhood B pose further challenges. A staggering 23 percent of housing units are vacant. High rates of housing vacancy are positively associated with increased crime, risk of fire, and drug use. Housing vacancy also increases property maintenance and decreases home values in nearby areas, thereby reducing household wealth overall.

Food establishments in Neighborhood B are not considered healthy food retailers, which is a source of concern because lack of access to healthy food is associated with health problems and obesity in children. Further, the availability of nearby health care facilities ranks in the lowest 25 percent of all neighborhoods in the metropolitan area.

hoods are African American (66%) and Hispanic (59%). By contrast, most children living in places like Neighborhood A are non-Hispanic White (66%) and Asian (62%). These calculations are based on the Child Opportunity Index, which measures neighborhood opportunities that help children develop.[37]

Another troubling consideration is that the disadvantage of living in places like Neighborhood B influences outcomes across generations.

Patrick Sharkey, a professor at Princeton University, has shown that living in a Neighborhood B over two generations is particularly damaging to those residents' cognitive skills. Second-generation children living in high-poverty neighborhoods score significantly lower on tests. And again, this disadvantage has a powerful racial inequality aspect to it. Almost half of all Black families have lived in poor neighborhoods over at least two generations, compared to 7 percent of white families. "If we want to understand how neighborhoods and cities alter the trajectories of families, it is essential to consider the types of environments in which families live over long periods of time and over an extended period of a family's history," according to Sharkey.[38] He argues that "the story of racial inequality in the current generation must be thought of as a continuation of a story that extends well back in time." And he concludes, "To truly understand inequality in America, then, it is necessary to move beyond a focus on income, occupation, and education, the traditional markers of socioeconomic status, and to consider the ways in which inequality is organized in space."[39]

Finally, no fact speaks more powerfully to how neighborhoods shape our future and our health than the research showing that when low-income kids move from low-opportunity neighborhoods to high-opportunity ones, their chances of escaping poverty improve dramatically.[40] And research by Chetty and others demonstrates that moving from a Neighborhood B to a Neighborhood A contributes to a number of improved outcomes, ranging from better test scores to improved physical and mental health.

What Does It Take to Make More Salutogenic Neighborhoods?

All communities everywhere need the guardrails of a middle-class/high-opportunity neighborhood. This is not just a question of fairness—although it is that; it is also a smart move economically. Resourced neighborhoods are "a garden for the growing of people" as community

FIGURE 2.3   Framework for Neighborhoods That Support Health and Financial Wellbeing[42]

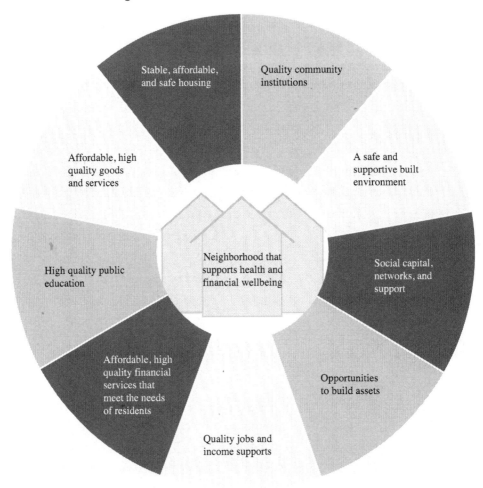

developer pioneer Jim Rouse used to say.[41] And these gardens bear the fruit of engaged and productive citizens. At a time when economists struggle to understand why productivity in our country has leveled off, this is a surefire way to engage the underutilized talents of nearly a fifth of our country who do not live in the communities that allow them to reach their potential.

Anyone reading this book can reflect on their own life and think of the many hundreds of things that went right in their life that allowed them to progress and overcome the many obstacles we all encounter over a lifetime. The one teacher in high school who made you think you were more capable than you thought you were. The reference librarian who taught you how to use the *Readers' Guide to Periodical Literature* (what we used before Google) so you could finish that term paper and experience the pride of overcoming an academic hurdle. The coach who stayed with you after practice and helped you perfect your free-throw shooting. These mentors could come from many places—Sunday School teacher, den mother, minister, big brother/big sister, and many others who helped you build confidence.

You can't plan how this support will arrive in your life. It arrives like Easter eggs found in unlikely places. Overlapping and sustained support such as this creates an ecosystem that nurtures children. And if those institutions and mentors are not present, support at critical and unexpected times is not available. The environment is not nurturing in that case; it tends to push people toward the toxic stress described by Shonkoff and his colleagues.

Our efforts to provide additional levels of support to struggling communities through narrow social programs have failed. The strategy of sprinkling a few amenities in a neighborhood through a series of "programs" (community development, Title I, SNAP, etc.) has not worked. Even relatively successful programs, such as the Harlem Children's Zone, cannot quite replicate the effectiveness of a more organically developed nurturing ecosystem.

Neighborhoods like A and B described earlier represent thousands of other neighborhoods in every city, and in every region, of the country. Neighborhood A is a nurturing ecosystem that has the zone defense that promotes health. The task before us is to build more guardrails in Neighborhood Bs and provide the proper incentives in those neighborhoods for social-airbag providers to intervene at critical moments to boost the outcomes in those low-opportunity places.

Building a Nurturing Ecosystem Requires Guardrails and Airbags, Not Grand Plans and Specific Programs

In a famous exchange between Jim Rouse, mentioned earlier, and Jane Jacobs, the liberal icon and author of *The Death and Life of Great American Cities*, Jacobs challenged Rouse's concept of bold big programs and designed communities. Communities, she said, developed organically. The exchange was described in a *Washington Post* article: "At the conference, Rouse approvingly quoted the famous words of architect Daniel Burnham: 'Make no little plans, for they have no magic to stir men's blood.'" Jacobs responded: "Funny, big plans never stirred women's blood. Women have always been willing to consider little plans." She brought down the house.[43]

"Big plans" and social programs rely on linear thinking—the step-by-step approach that allows for a series of actions that lead to the ultimate desired conclusion. Sending a spacecraft to Mars is hard, but it basically involves millions of actions with known outcomes. Using a rocket to get the spacecraft there requires following those steps. "Little plans," in Jacobs's assessment, are the thousands of nurturing acts over childhood, for example, which add up to a prepared adult. There is no plan for these interventions, they are the result of a nurturing ecosystem, or what I described earlier as a zone defense. And they can be better understood by using complex adaptive systems thinking.

Complex adaptive systems are ones that are self-organizing and have a number of rules that help explain how they operate (feedback loops, tipping points, etc.). These rules are also important to the operation of guardrails and airbags as these interventions try to achieve outcomes such as a child ready to learn at kindergarten, a student graduating from high school, or a formerly homeless person who is stably housed. To be effective, many organizations must work in concert across sectors and silos to achieve those outcomes without a central planner. Success depends on fertile ground (a neighborhood with guardrails) and the right combination of airbags deploying at the right times across the life course.[44] That is why a paradigm shift from linear thinking (single programs, or big plans) must give way to complex adaptive system thinking (organic development, nurturing ecosystems, or little plans).

Sometimes the term *complex adaptive system* can put readers off because it signals something "too complex" to tackle, but there can be simplicity in this concept. In essence, complex systems are ones that have no central planner, and yet they achieve amazing results. There are examples in many varied settings. In nature, army ants basically do three things: (1) find food, (2) build and maintain a nest, and (3) protect the queen. One army ant alone would simply die. But hundreds of thousands of ants working together create elaborate communities and thrive. Similarly, T cells in our bodies are basically able to do only three things: (1) determine if a cell in our bodies is "us" or "not us," (2) if it is not us, take notes on its details, and (3) help other parts of the immune system create neutralizers for the "not us" intruder. With those simple rules, T cells protect our bodies from harmful intruders every day. Similarly, consumers in a market—be that a grocery store or the New York Stock Exchange—make purchasing decisions based on perceived quality and price. Those simple decisions drive trillions of dollars of investment, production, and sales every day. All three examples are complex adaptive systems, and yet they rest on fairly simple decision rules.[45]

The relevance here is that we could use a complex adaptive system approach by creating clear end goals (outcomes) that allow intersecting approaches to achieving those goals. For example, I often cite the goal of a child ready to learn at kindergarten. To get that child there—eager and ready to learn on the first day of school—many organizations must work in concert across sectors and silos to achieve the outcomes without a central planner. Success depends not on centralized authority but, rather, fertile ground (a neighborhood with guardrails) and the right combination of airbags over the life course.[46] Success doesn't necessarily rely on a detailed plan. Instead, like the

T cells, hundreds of organizations will be executing on thousands of interventions that together provide that child the support, encouragement, and enrichment to succeed.

Airbags Complement Guardrails to Create a Nurturing Ecosystem to Bridge Kids into Adulthood

If guardrails are place-based institutions/features/organizations that help make a neighborhood function well and promote growth, wellbeing, and health, then airbags are the people-based interventions that help individuals at critical times to either mitigate damage done from bad circumstances or perhaps even learn, grow, and become stronger as a result of them. Airbags tend to be social services like the tutoring or counseling mentioned earlier. They can be legal support, coaching, music lessons, drug rehab, Outward Bound wilderness experiences, and many other interventions that help people—children in particular—develop into well-equipped adults. Putnam describes social airbags in his book *Our Kids* in the following way: "Studies during the past 40 years have consistently shown that, if anything, drug usage and binge drinking are more common among privileged teenagers than among their less affluent peers. What is different, however, are the family and community 'air bags' that deploy to minimize the negative consequences of drugs and other misadventures among rich kids."[47]

The lack of airbags contributes to the achievement gap among children that is apparent in kindergarten, according to Putnam, and predictably grows worse over time. The negative consequences of this can snowball over the course of childhood. By the time children are applying to college, if they get that far, the disparity is stark. "High-scoring poor kids are now slightly less likely (29 percent) to get a college degree than low-scoring rich kids (30 percent)," according to Putnam. Part of the explanation, according to Putnam, is substantial advantage that affluent kids have in informal mentoring. "[N]early two thirds of affluent kids (64 percent) have some mentoring beyond their extended family, while nearly two thirds of poor kids (62 percent) do not."[48] And in addition to fewer mentors, poor kids have less robust social networks, especially the valuable "weak ties" that were first described by Stanford sociologist Mark Granovetter. Weak ties are the connections you might have through your swim team, sorority, or soccer club and are the ones that extend your reach in terms of ideas and important information, such as job leads.[49]

The idea of "bridging" young people into adulthood is an idea that is more familiar than you might suspect. For example, why do you think so many colleges are located in faraway places—forests like my alma mater Dartmouth College, or small towns strewn about rural America? These are places where you are less likely to get into trouble as you make decisions guided by the "hyperbolic preferences," as described by economists, of one's youth. Many countries require mandatory military services of young men, and while there are elements of national defense in that policy, it is also an effective way to keep young men from getting into trouble.

Airbags are critical for getting kids and young adults past the rocks and whirlpools that life throws at them. Brookings researchers Ron Haskins and Isabel Sawhill argue that if you can avoid three potential traps in your youth, you are almost certain to avoid living in poverty. The three things to avoid poverty are (1) finish high school, (2) have no more than two children after you are 21 years old and married, and (3) work full time at a job. According to Haskins and Sawhill, "The poverty rate among families with children could be lowered by 71 percent if the poor completed high school, worked full-time, married, and had no more than two children."[50]

Those three things sound simple, but we know that they are not. All three of those outcomes require thousands of things to go right in the life of a child and young adult. And the obstacles to those things going right are legion: multigenerational poverty, institutional racism, and a biased criminal justice system that marks formerly convicted people and makes it harder to find a well-paying, entry-level job. Add to these barriers that a changing economy has fewer low-skilled man-ufacturing and other entry-level jobs. Even so, they are at least goals to aim at. And it is less daunting than trying to tackle the many structural forces that we often hear must be tackled: capitalism, rac-ism, or the many factors that Thomas Piketty describes in *Capital in the Twenty-First Century* that drive the growing wealth gap.

I think structural barriers are serious problems. I think the grow-ing wealth gap is a serious problem, and I know that smart policymak-ers and researchers are working on them. What I am arguing here is that let's also work on the little plans that nurture kids so that we can begin to level an unequal playing field. It is not all that needs to be done, but it is an important start.

There Are Many Examples of Airbags

One way to imagine how airbags work is to consider them from a human-centered design standpoint—a perspective that focuses on the end user. Consider a pregnant first-time mother who needs support. Coaching about parenting a newborn and getting the home and family ready to receive the baby could be done by an organization such as the Nurse Family Partnership, an airbag helping that first-time mom have the best experience possible with her newborn baby.

In the 1990s, pediatric researchers Betty Hart and Todd Risley[51] found that lower-income children hear 30 million fewer words by the age of 3 than middle-income children, with this difference account-ing for meaningful differences in language development and how these children fared in school.[52] An airbag here could be early, high-quality childhood enrichment classes, such as the well-studied Perry Pre-school, Abecedarian Project, Chicago Child–Parent Centers, or other high-quality preschool programs demonstrated to have resulted in sub-stantial positive results for kids over a lifetime.[53]

Preschool teachers who get to know their students in these settings are in a good position to trigger an airbag if they notice an obstacle to learning, such as poor vision, or might detect budding developmental problems, or adverse issues in the child's home. There are a number of adults who touch and influence the lives of children who would also be in a position to trigger an airbag intervention, including elementary school teachers, librarians, bus drivers, and crossing guards.

We have already seen how mentorship is critically important to a child's development. But having an adult who is not your parent but who cares about you is a similar type of ever-present airbag. Thanks to the research of Emmy Werner, a University of California, Davis, professor, who has been following cohorts of children over generations on the island of Kauai in Hawaii, we now know that kids in similar circumstances with this steadying presence tend to be more successful and healthier.[54]

There are a number of interventions that incorporate the wonder and challenge of interacting with nature as a strategy to focus kids on building their own self-confidence. One of the oldest is Boy and Girl Scouts. Outward Bound is an outdoor education experience that strives to impart self-awareness, self-confidence, leadership skills, and environmental and social responsibility.[55] Another example, building on the idea of the Civilian Conservation Corp (CCC) of the New Deal, is the CCC in California, which takes young people out into the many beautiful wilderness areas of California to build trails, engage in fire protection and other natural disaster response, and create more opportunities for individuals to experience the wonder of California's wild places. The motto of the CCC is "hard work, low pay, miserable conditions, and more!" but that kidding aside, it promises participants the opportunity to learn skills in firefighting and environmental resource protection, make new friends, and earn college scholarships.[56]

The arts are such a powerful tool for creating deeper understanding of the world around us and for personal growth. Arts and artists, like many sectors, are both guardrails and airbags. The ways in which they operate as airbags are numerous, ranging from the high school play that kept one young girl engaged in her school, which I mentioned in the introduction, to the muralist in San Francisco who helped a group of African American and Latinx kids heal their divide in the Bay View Hunters Point neighborhood through a series of wall murals they co-created.[57]

Many of us carry the deep-seated lessons we learned as participants in sports—teamwork, discipline, diligence, and learning to win but especially how to lose. There should be no barriers to participating in as many sports as possible. We need to provide the funding for coaches, equipment, transportation, and other supports to create the infrastructure for a thriving sports culture in all neighborhoods—especially in places similar to Neighborhood B described earlier.

Serving others is a gift to the one who receives the service and the one who gives it. It taps into a deep need to feel useful and provides a sense of purpose. As Martin Luther King Jr., in a sermon at the Ebenezer Baptist Church in Atlanta, told the congregation, "Everybody can be great, because everyone can serve."[58] Providing people the encouragement and opportunity to volunteer their time and talents to their neighbors is a great way to help the volunteers too—by providing them with structure and the satisfaction of making a difference. There is also a fair amount of evidence that volunteering "facilitates social integration, distraction from one's troubles, a sense of meaning, self-efficacy, positive mood, and physical activity, all of which may promote health," according to University of Buffalo researcher Michael Poulin.[59]

Providing service to others is closely connected to the idea of finding a spiritual home. Again, this is a topic that is both guardrail (churches, synagogues, mosques, temples, meditation centers) and airbag (guidance from spiritual leaders in difficult times). This is such a challenge in our time. We disagree on what it means to have this type of support. But the need for it is profound. Early theories about the construction of religious buildings and temples in prehistoric times theorized that these buildings were constructed after humans started agriculture and could support living in larger towns and cities about

10,000 years ago. It is interesting that recent archaeological evidence suggests that humans were building temples before they built cities. The need for spiritual homes predated our need for actual homes.[60]

My grandfather used to encourage me to travel; "it broadens one," he used to say. That exploration gives new perspectives and gets us out of our own heads. And as T. S. Eliot reminds us, "We shall not cease from exploration. And the end of all our exploring. Will be to arrive where we started. And know the place for the first time."[61] Therefore student exchange programs like American Field Service or Youth for Understanding are important airbags for young people who are struggling to understand their place in our society and our world.

Other setbacks to avoid during one's youth include committing a crime—especially a violent one—and any entanglement with the police and criminal justice system. Arrest rates for violent offenses spike before age 24 and then decline.[62] Getting young men through that period is critical to getting them into adulthood. Finding ways to engage young men in constructive challenges is an important strategy to improve overall societal health. It is worth noting, however, that the threat from violent crime has decreased substantially in almost all American cities since a highwater mark in the 1970s, "in many cases by more than 75 percent," according to Sharkey.[63] This is true for both Neighborhood A and B.

A job is one of the most powerful social determinants of health and getting one for disadvantaged people can be hard—especially those who have struggled with mental health issues, homelessness, or incarceration. That is why an airbag like the nonprofit Roberts Enterprise Development Fund (REDF) is critical. REDF is a social enterprise that helps disadvantaged people get trained for jobs. But more than just training, they own a fleet of social enterprises that are operated as a business (as caterers, restaurants, dog daycare, cleaning crews, etc.) where the goal is to make money *and* provide a welcoming environment for workers who are learning how to be part of the private-sector workforce. Those employers provide extra help and support so their employees can grow into the job and get more confident as contributors to the business. An airbag like a job from REDF is especially helpful for those returning to their community from prison, young people who ran away from home, and people who were formerly homeless. Since 1997, REDF has supported the growth and success of over two hundred employment social enterprises in more than thirty states. These social enterprises have earned over $1.3 billion in revenue and employed over 84,000 people.[64]

Finally, education is obviously a powerful force in all our lives. Like other topics, it is both guardrail (well-funded and high-performing schools) and airbag (tutoring, early childhood enrichment, special education). The economic consequences of getting a good education, and especially a college degree, are getting starker. According to research by the economist David Autor, between 1980 and 2012, "the hourly earnings of full-time college-educated males rose anywhere from 20 percent to 56 percent." Males with a high school education or less saw their incomes decline over the same period—22 percent for high school dropouts and 11 percent for high school graduates.[65] I have touched on the many airbags in this category—tutoring, summer school catch-up classes, career coaching, school counseling are all examples of important education-related airbags. But given the fact that the penalty for low-education outcomes is getting harsher, we must redouble our efforts to improve opportunity in this category.

Data, Predictive Analytics, and Complex Adaptive Systems

The two essential elements that can bring this system of airbags to life are data and money. I tackle how we pay for these interventions in chapter 3, but the interventions do not work unless, like the car's airbag, the sensors are working.

There are many efforts to build a data infrastructure for neighborhoods. Here are just a few examples:

City Health Dashboard Developed by New York University Langone Medical School, the dashboard allows researchers to see where cities across the United States stand on over thirty-five measures of health and factors affecting health across five areas: Health Behaviors, Social and Economic Factors, Physical Environment, Health Outcomes, and Clinical Care. Recently, the Federal Reserve Bank of New York has teamed up with NYU to provide more economic and access-to-credit data to the dashboard. Available at www.cityhealthdashboard.com/.

Opportunity Insights Based at Harvard University, a team of researchers and policy analysts work together to analyze new data and create a platform for local stakeholders to make more informed decisions. Available at https://opportunityinsights.org/.

Opportunity Atlas In a collaboration with Raj Chetty and Nathan Hendren from Harvard University and John Friedman from Brown University, the U.S. Census constructed the Opportunity Atlas, a comprehensive census tract–level dataset of children's outcomes in adulthood using data covering nearly the entire U.S. population. Each tract has estimates of children's outcomes in adulthood, such as earnings distributions and incarceration rates by parental income, race, and gender. Available at www.census.gov/programs-surveys/ces/data/analysis-visualiza tion-tools/opportunity-atlas.html.

U.S. Small-Area Life Expectancy Estimates Project This project is a partnership of the CDC's National Center for Health Statistics, the Robert Wood Johnson Foundation, and the National Association for Public Health Statistics and Information Systems to produce a new measure of health for where you live. The project produced estimates of life expectancy at birth—the average number of years a person can expect to live—for most of the census tracts in the United States for the period 2010–2015. Available at www.cdc.gov/nchs/nvss /usaleep/usaleep.html#data.

Community Commons This is a collaborative initiative spearheaded by the Institute for People, Place, and Possibility that helps change-makers advance equitable community health and wellbeing using the best tools, resources, data, and stories to support their work. Available at www.communitycommons.org/.

Opportunity360 Created and maintained by Enterprise Community Partners, Opportunity 360 is a comprehensive approach to understanding and addressing community challenges by identifying pathways to greater opportunities using cross-sector data, community engagement, and measurement tools. With this insight, partners in community development will be better positioned to make smart investments and create collaborative solutions that transform communities across the country. Available at www.enterprisecommunity.org/opportunity360\.

National Neighborhood Indicators Project This learning network, coordinated by the Urban Institute, connects independent partner organizations in more than thirty cities that share a mission to ensure that all communities have access to data and the skills to use information to advance equity and wellbeing across neighborhoods. Available at www.neighborhoodindicators .org/about-nnip.

Child Opportunity Index An index of neighborhood resources and conditions that helps children develop in a healthy way, the Child Opportunity Index combines data from twenty-nine neighborhood-level indicators into a single composite measure. Established in 2014 with support from the W.K. Kellogg Foundation and the Robert Wood Johnson Foundation, diver sitydatakids.org set out to fill an urgent need for a rigorous, equity-focused research program with a clear mission to help improve child wellbeing and increase racial and ethnic equity in opportunities for children. This index (http://new.diversity datakids.org/child-opportunity-index) was the basis for the profiles of high-opportunity Neighborhood A and low-opportunity Neighborhood B in this chapter.

These data platforms are a recent breakthrough. They could be a good start as we build the capability to establish baselines and measure progress of airbag and guardrail interventions.

In addition to having access to data at the neighborhood level, we also need data on an individual level. There are many strategies that could be useful here. Simply collecting school grades is a start. In instances where grades are falling it would raise a flag that there might be trouble. If we commit to this type of data gathering, there will be more innovations in this arena.

The data are not helpful unless the analysis is fast, reliable, and accurate. Here we might rely on artificial intelligence, predictive analytics, and machine learning to create the types of analysis that anticipate needs and help time the interventions in a way that matches the accuracy of an automobile's airbag sensors.

Dena Bravata is a medical doctor and health researcher who is also a serial entrepreneur and venture investor for companies that "make healthcare better and more affordable for all," as she states on her Twitter profile. Dr. Bravata has helped launch several companies over the years. One in particular, Lyra Health, focuses on mental health services and recently passed a milestone of serving its 100,000th patient.[66] Dr. Bravata has researched Lyra's claims data to see what would predict the need for treatment of depression or anxiety. Some findings were not surprising; patients who needed mental health treatment in year two often had serious health shocks in year one—heart attack, breast cancer, and so forth. What was more surprising to Dr. Bravata was that patients who had regular preventive dental exams but began skipping those visits in year one were just as likely as those with massive health shocks to need mental health treatment in year two. It seems like an odd early sign, but as you begin to lose interest in your oral health, there is an indication that more serious problems are lurking.

I once asked a Mormon friend what happens when someone of his faith was known to be doing something forbidden like drinking alcohol or caffeinated coffee. His response was that the person would be greeted with a lot of "fellowship" from his fellow parishioners. What if a person who missed a dentist appointment, had a sudden drop in their grades, or some other sign of stress was greeted with a lot of fellowship too? This type of intervention would be in the spirit of offering support and would not be a formal investigation or punitive intervention. A dose of "fellowship," delivered at the right time, is an airbag.

How the data and analysis are used to coordinate, guide, align, and integrate multiple airbag interventions is a challenge. But here, too, we have some examples that can point the way to what is possible. William Gibson said, "The future is here, it's just unevenly distributed." There are examples of how a tech platform that is web based and data driven can help execute on multiagency, wraparound interventions for vulnerable people.

One such platform is Unite US, which was created originally to enhance the services and case management of physical and mental health needs of veterans and now uses that platform for wider communities of patients with integrated health systems, such as Kaiser Permanente. The platform aligns "stakeholders from healthcare, government, and the community around a shared goal to improve health," according to the company's website. "Our proven infrastructure provides both a person-centered care coordination platform and a hands-on community engagement process; we work hand-in-hand with communities to ensure services are seamlessly delivered to the people who need them most."[67] Unite US facilitates communication and coordination of care across multiple service providers. Perhaps most importantly, it tracks critical data that allow the network to learn and improve its interventions for each client.

Privacy and Opting-In

I recognize that all of this can seem a bit like Big Brother in George Orwell's dystopian novel, *1984*. There would never be a mandate for individuals and families to participate in the airbag system. Although I do think it should be an opt-in system that encourages people to participate, at least on a trial basis. And I do believe if we could get a few prototype communities up and running and could show the value of these interventions, it would convince others of the value of them. In the end, I don't think many parents (especially those who are feeling overwhelmed) would object to a second line of defense keeping their children on a productive path toward adulthood.

There are many ways we could build privacy protections into this system. How much privacy people really require is an open question since many of us respond to surveys to say that privacy is important while simultaneously using apps and search engines that track our every move on the internet, phones and home smart devices listen to our conversations, and increasingly we post every move on social media. Nevertheless, I think using blockchain technology has the dual benefit of creating a hack-proof backbone to a case management system for every child that allows multiple airbag providers to come in and out of a child's file without compromising that individual's privacy. Blockchain technology, the secure open-ledger software, could be a powerful tool to enable an airbag system to achieve the coordination and alignment that are hinted at by a technology platform like Unite US.

Guardrails and Airbags Are Not Free: How to Pay for Them

None of this is cheap. But doing nothing is also expensive. As I argued in the introduction, there is a lot of money in the multiple systems—health care, antipoverty, community development, education, criminal justice and incarceration—that are currently uncoordinated and too focused on downstream Band-Aid interventions. Those resources could be repurposed for upstream investments that promote health and wellbeing. Tapping into the resources unleashed by the twin revolutions of outcomes-based financing for antipoverty policy and population-health business models that pay for health rather than medical care are the themes I will tackle in chapter 3.

CHAPTER 3

Financing Guardrails and Airbags

Creating a Market That Values Health

GUARDRAILS AND AIRBAGS ARE WHERE THE RUBBER meets the road. They are where health is created because they are the moments where dreams are kept alive, where kids feel supported and nurtured, and where good options are available so that the healthy choice is the easy choice. A lot of money can be directed to these elements of neighborhoods (guardrails) or interventions in an individual's life (airbags) if we are creative on two fronts: (1) increasing the effectiveness of the money we currently spend inefficiently in neighborhoods, on social welfare, and on the negative consequences of poverty; and (2) redirecting what we currently spend on avoidable, downstream medical care costs to invest instead on addressing the upstream drivers of poor health. The creative breakthroughs that make this possible are Pay for Success strategies for social welfare spending and population health business models to spend more on the upstream determinants of health. Together these two sources of financing for guardrails and airbags create what I am calling the "market that values health."[1]

Economic historians know that almost all markets are created in response to demand pressure. As Adam Smith observed over two hundred years ago, "It is not the multitude of ale-houses . . . that occasions a general disposition to drunkenness among the common people; but that disposition [to drunkenness] arising from other causes necessarily gives employment to a multitude of ale-houses."[2] The demand that could support a market that values health is staggering. We currently spend $393 billion yearly on antipoverty programs (this excludes money spent on health care for Americans living in poverty).[3] And there are substantial additional resources spent each year to improve low-income communities, such as the hundreds of billions of dollars invested annually in response to the Community Reinvestment Act. (Analysis from the Urban Institute estimated that over $400 billion in lending and investing "counted" toward CRA obligations.)[4] Redirecting a small percentage of those resources to upstream interventions could jumpstart demand for more guardrails and airbags. And money that is now spent on the chronic diseases caused by living in poverty could be redirected upstream too. Dr. Jutte estimates that amount in the following way: "In the U.S. we currently spend at least $3.5 trillion per year on healthcare. Over 85% of those resources are spent on chronic disease, and we know that a substantial portion of chronic disease is preventable, linked to poverty, and concentrated in low-income communities. This translates to at least $1 trillion spent annually on avoidable chronic disease among residents of low-income neighborhoods."[5]

In addition to these two sources of demand, the market that values health will need some fast and flexible money in the early stages of its development, especially grants from foundations and other sources.

A robust market that values health may seem too good to be true, but not if you recognize that the status quo is inefficient and extremely expensive. Focusing on the upstream social determinants of health, which requires very common-sense approaches to nurturing people, has eye-popping money-saving potential. Addressing these upstream interventions helps everyone, but the impacts are substantially greater for low-income people and communities.

When more than a trillion dollars starts flowing to provide more guardrails and airbags, the market that values health will spread and scale. This new demand will attract new actors who will innovate with new business models. The entrepreneurs who innovate and succeed will have both problem-solving skills and a deep understanding of the community they serve. This combination almost guarantees that the teams that respond to improve a community's health will reflect the racial, ethnic, language, cultural, gender, sexual identity, and other characteristics of their community. No intervention can create positive change if it is solely initiated by outsiders, even those with the best intentions.

The Market That Values Health Is Modeled on Community Development Finance

The market that values health is modeled on an earlier innovation in how we provide community development interventions to create more amenities, such as affordable housing, schools, and clinics, to low-income neighborhoods that was developed in the 1960s–1980s. Both markets are really "quasi-markets" because both depend significantly on government subsidies in the form of grant dollars or low-interest loans to provide the effective demand that drives the system, at least initially, rather than depending solely on private-sector demand. As described in chapter 1, community development, which finances the real estate assets every community needs (clinics, schools, housing, etc.), may not seem that similar to the buyers, producers, and connectors in the market that values health, but these two quasi-markets resonate in powerful ways.

The community development sector arose as a response to prior eras when large bureaucracies, such as the Department of Housing and Urban Development, were responsible for investing in struggling communities. Top-down bureaucracies based in Washington, DC, were not well positioned to plan and execute the complicated revitalization strategy for communities across the country. Not only were all those communities unique with community-specific needs, but there was also no way to keep up with the rapidly evolving circumstances on the ground. In other words, there was no "sense and respond" capability with these interventions. Spending a lot of money on auto pilot is a bad idea for many reasons, chief among them is that the right decisions in time period one are almost never appropriate for time periods two or three. Needs change over time.

An advantage of this quasi-market approach to neighborhood investing as it developed in the 1980s and 1990s was that it allowed local actors—community development corporations (CDCs), community development financial institutions (CDFIs), community-based organizations (CBOs)—to respond to local conditions and tap into larger federal subsidy dollars—the investment tax credit programs (Low Income Housing Tax Credit and New Markets Tax Credit Program) along with the block grant programs to states and local governments. In many cases, the neighborhood resources these groups were building—low-rent apartment buildings, grocery stores, clinics, childcare centers, and schools—would generate revenue from residents, customers, or patients paying for rent, groceries, or care, and students through per-pupil funding.

The government subsidies in the form of tax incentives and grants, however, tipped projects that were "near bankable" into ones that were "bankable," meaning that they became financially feasible and were built. Because these investments were businesses, they required hard-headed financial discipline to get them over the finish line. That feature had an added benefit; these projects were not solely beholden to government or philanthropic handouts. They could also tap the commercial capital markets for financing.

Like the work of the community development sector, the market that values health will also have its demand boosted by government subsidies. Pay for Success contracts, and population health investments—especially in places where the government owns the downstream medical care cost risk—will also drive demand. It will develop a number of new interventions and organizations similar to CDCs, CDFIs, and CBOs. And it will use many of the market-connector strategies used in community development, including CDFIs, social impact bonds, CRA-motivated financing, capital stacks, and the like.

Buying More Health with a Population Health Business Model

The need to focus on the root drivers of health, like control of destiny or hope, is gaining traction in health and medical circles. There is growing evidence that managing social needs upstream can create savings downstream by avoiding medical costs. A recent review of the scientific research in *Health Affairs* concluded that "healthy choices in homes, neighborhoods, schools, and workplaces can have decisive impacts on health." The review concluded that interventions on the social determinants of health "can improve population health and reduce health disparities." And that these interventions "lead to long-term societal savings." The article acknowledges, however, that those savings are hard to capture and hard to finance.[6]

One development is making these interventions more plausible—the new financing arrangements, such as "capitation," "global budgeting," Accountable Care Organizations (ACOs), Accountable Care Communities (ACCs), Accountable Communities for Health (ACHs), and other alternative payment models that "require population health management and strategies for reducing utilization," according to Jacqueline LaPointe, editor at Xtelligent Healthcare Media.[7] These population-health interventions improve efficiency and coordination of care to keep a population of patients healthy at a lower cost. ACCs are an even more comprehensive effort to address "a critical gap between clinical care and community services in the current health care delivery system," according to Centers for Medicare and Medicaid

Services. They do this by "systematically identifying and addressing the health-related social needs of Medicare and Medicaid beneficiaries through screening, referral, and community navigation services [that] will impact health care costs and reduce health care utilization."[8]

Many of the value-based payment models focus on coordinating medical care, and while that is important, it does not often go the additional step to tackle the upstream drivers of care. Efforts such as ACCs are attempting to make that jump to population-health management.[9] There are twenty-nine ACCs across the country. The preliminary research on the effectiveness of this effort to screen beneficiaries and help them navigate social services is inconclusive other than some reduction of emergency department visits, but these are still very early days for the program.[10]

The costs from vulnerable people who are "frequent flyers" and high utilizers of medical care are well known. An analysis by Advocate Health Care, for example, found that malnourished patients cost nearly twice as much as well-nourished peers because they are in the hospital longer and have higher readmission rates. A Chicago hospital found that 200 of its chronically homeless patients were among its most expensive, with annual per-patient expenses ranging from $51,000 to $533,000.[11] The focus on food security, affordable housing, and transportation often results in significant cost savings when treating vulnerable patients. The Commonwealth Fund developed a "Health ROI Calculator." This creative and helpful tool for health payers estimates savings from better managing the social determinants of health care of high-need, high-cost patients "who account for a large share of overall health care spending." These patients, they observe, "often have social needs, clinically complex conditions, cognitive or physical limitations, and/or behavioral health problems."[12]

But in a blog for Health Affairs, Brian Castrucci and John Auerbach argue that meeting social needs (e.g., food or housing insecurity) of high utilizers of medical care is popular and provides cost savings, but does not go far enough upstream to root causes. "While health care leaders have realized that programs to buy food, offer temporary housing, or cover ridesharing programs are less expensive than providing repeat health care services for their highest cost patients, such patient-centered assistance does not improve the underlying social and economic factors that affect the health of everyone in a community."[13]

In a river analogy, it is essential to pull drowning people out as they float by. But it is equally important to go upstream and stop more people from falling into the river in the first place. "This isn't about picking one approach over another," according to Castrucci and Auerbach. "We need social and economic interventions at both the community and individual levels." Failing to tackle root causes upstream means more patients (and more expensive patients) downstream. The incentives to focus upstream grow stronger, they conclude, "as the movement to Accountable Health Communities and value-based care gains momentum."[14]

Making sure that people do not fall into the river in the first place is the inspiration for guardrails and airbag interventions. It relies on a more aggressive and systemic effort to instill a sense of control over one's destiny, pride in one's community, and hope. Finding ways to pay for this will require many reforms like paying for health promotion rather than medical care as in the ACO, ACC, and other value-based care examples mentioned earlier.

Health systems are demonstrating how they can simultaneously pay for medical care and invest in the upstream social determinants of health. Between 2017 and 2019, health systems spent $2.5 billion on upstream issues, according to a study in the journal *Health Affairs*. Most of that spending was on housing interventions ($1.6 billion) followed by employment ($1.1 billion), education ($476 million), food security ($294 million), social and community context ($253 million), and transportation ($32 million).[15]

The health systems on the vanguard of this holistic approach to improving health are health insurers that are also medical care providers. Kaiser Permanente was an early pioneer in this approach, known in the medical field as integrated systems. An article in *Becker's Hospital Review* listed one hundred of these integrated health systems across the country (and it was not an exhaustive list): "The health systems listed here focus on the continuum of care, from wellness and preventive services to urgent care, inpatient care, outpatient care, hospice, health plan offerings and more. Many of these health systems have also demonstrated innovation through their participation in care and payment reform initiatives, such as accountable care organizations."[16]

The incentives of these integrated systems are exactly in line with the market that values health.

As the preceding discussion illustrates, health systems are migrating into this buyer category to improve health. But they could be sped along by the massive purchasing power of government at all levels (federal, state, and local) in the medical care market. Of course, buying medical care does not necessarily buy health, but it is a gauge of what is possible if we reorient some of that spending to start focusing upstream. In 2020, Americans spent over $4 trillion in medical care (a significant increase over the prior year thanks to the pandemic). The largest purchaser of medical care was the federal government (36.3 percent) followed closely by households (26.1 percent), according to data from Centers for Medicare and Medicaid Services. Private businesses spent 16.7 percent followed by state and local governments at 14.3 percent. An additional 7.5 percent was spent from other private sources.[17] Government, then, paid nearly $2 trillion in 2019 for medical care.[18] Given this massive scale of spending, it seems likely that there will be places where government is almost a single payer— where it "owns" the downstream medical care cost risk. In these places, government is poised to be a substantial "buyer" of upstream social determinants of health interventions as a strategy to avoid some of its downstream medical care cost.

Leaders in the health and medical field see the move to population health business models as the future of the industry. It is impossible to create better health outcomes by focusing on access to and quality of medical care. That is why Tyler Norris, president of the Well Being Trust (a foundation created by the Providence St. Joseph Health system), and his coauthor Jme McLean, call for "initiatives that focus on resilient and equitable community development—safe affordable housing, active and accessible transportation options, healthy and affordable food, economic opportunity, and quality education, particularly in historically disinvested communities where health outcomes tend to be worse and threats of climate change are greatest—are critical, upstream drivers of health. Deeper investments in these non-health-care drivers of health outcomes are needed to improve health outcomes and slow the growth of health care costs."[19] Even though these are early days, the chorus of voices calling for this move to upstream investments by the health sector are growing louder.[20]

Buying More Health with Pay for Success Finance

Another substantial source of demand for buying better health outcomes could come from redirecting dollars currently earmarked for the social service sector. Pay for Success and outcomes-based financing strategies are ways to redirect some of these dollars. The use of funds outside the current system of social service payments is also necessary to build the new system while we continue to maintain the old one. Tools like the social impact bond will be particularly key here, where impact investors will take the risk on new upstream guardrail and airbag approaches to improve social outcomes in a community.

In 2017, the Federal Reserve Bank of San Francisco and the Nonprofit Finance Fund brought eighty authors together to write fifty-five essays on Pay for Success—also referred to as outcomes-based financing—in the book *What Matters: Investing in Results to Build Strong, Vibrant Communities*.[21] This is the most comprehensive collection of essays on the topic, exploring social impact bonds, advance market commitments, rate cards, social impact insurance, and many others. In her summary chapter of that book, Andrea Levere, the former CEO of Prosperity Now, wrote that the central idea for the book "seems narrow: to convert how we structure, finance, operate, and evaluate the delivery of social services to an outcomes-based approach to achieve better results, maximize efficiencies, leverage new sources of capital, and achieve unprecedented levels of scale." But she cautions that this is misleading: "Yet its scope becomes as wide as human experience, as this approach is applied through 15 different tools to the work underway in at least a dozen sectors or specialties."[22]

Levere's insight captures this book as well. The argument here, too, is relatively simple and narrow in focus: support every baby in reaching adulthood using enrichment experiences, nurturing, support, and the tools they need to thrive over the life course. Making this happen is not simple and requires thousands of interventions that also span the "width of human experience." At the risk of oversimplification, I am summarizing those interventions as guardrails and airbags. But making these interventions operationally effective and paying for them will require complex Pay for Success and outcome-based financing.

To make this more concrete, consider the example of the first social impact bond in the United States. It was structured by Goldman Sachs with backing from New York City government and the Bloomberg Foundation to pay for a new approach to reducing juvenile prisoner recidivism at Rikers Island Correctional Center.[23] Nearly half of the juveniles detained in this jail are reincarcerated within one year of release. The intervention was intended to reduce that percentage to a lower rate (the successful outcome) by providing 3,000 16- to 18-year-old, formerly incarcerated youth with enhanced case management and social supports. While the intervention was successful in modestly reducing recidivism, the change did not meet the target goal. Investors lost their money because they did not achieve the agreed-upon outcome. Although the intervention was considered to be a failure, and investors never like to lose money, this effort served as an important experiment on how new interventions could be created, paid for by private-sector impact investors, evaluated for effectiveness, and shut down because of underperformance.[24] That rapid innovation and then moving on to new strategies is a powerful approach to getting to solutions, or what the tech industry describes as "failing fast" to get to the ultimate success. That is a useful way to improve social policy and a "win" in my opinion.

Tracy Palandjian, of Social Finance Inc., in her essay in *What Matters*, describes the design features baked into social impact bonds that "are predicated on aligned incentives for all involved stakeholders." She states that these financial mechanisms "allow governments to focus on preventive services, nonprofits to scale, and investors an opportunity to make an impact." Thus, according to Palandjian, social impact bonds do many things: they align multiple organizations around a goal, coordinate actions to achieve the goal, track and analyze progress, and pay for all those activities. Combining these features into a joint approach is remarkable in its design, and even though the results to date have been mixed, social impact bonds remain a potentially powerful tool to build the market that values health. And it is a flexible tool as well. Goldman Sachs also structured a social impact bond designed to help kids arrive at kindergarten ready to learn in Utah.[25] Another successful social impact bond helped finance supportive housing for formerly homeless individuals in Denver.[26] As we gain experience on how to use this finance tool, we might be able to tackle more complicated and longer-term outcomes, such as paying to keep children performing at grade level and graduating from high school.

The social impact bond features that inspire, align, track, and pay are also present in other Pay for Success tools. Prize-based philanthropy brought us many innovations, from the breakthroughs in ocean navigation in the 1700s to space tourism inspired by the Ansari XPRIZE.[27] This tool could also be used for social outcomes, as a team of authors from the XPRIZE Foundation wrote in their essay in *What Matters*, "The Power of Incentive Prize Competitions."[28] How about a prize for reducing, or eliminating, the race and class disparities in maternal and child health in the United States?

Not all outcomes-based finance tools have to be as complicated as the social impact bond. Rate cards used in the United Kingdom are relatively simple reimbursement rates determined by government agencies in return for achieving desired outcomes.[29] "All Pay for Success projects involve detailed work to identify a target population, select outcomes, and set a value for those outcomes," according to Andrew Levitt and Lara Metcalf in their *What Matters* essay. "But when Pay for Success projects are developed in response to an outcomes rate card, that work is front-loaded—government sets the prices, terms, and timeline before the procurement process." The simplicity of these linked goals (e.g., improved educational outcomes leading to placement in jobs) contributed to the success of the first round of interventions and has kept the experiment going to round two.

Some existing social finance tools could be tweaked to be more effective in the social outcomes realm. The Low Income Housing Tax Credit, for example, is already an effective outcomes-based financing tool to build affordable housing. This program, administered by the Internal Revenue Service (IRS), has built more homes for low-income people than the existing affordable housing built by all the federal housing programs that came before it.[30] The homes are high-quality, built on time and on budget, and the final tax benefits do not flow to the private-sector investors until the apartment building is complete and successfully leased up with low-income tenants who qualify for the reduced-rent apartments. When this is achieved, the IRS issues a Form 8609 to mark the successful outcome, which triggers the final payment to investors.[31] Terri Ludwig, president of Balmer Group Philanthropy, suggests we could build on the housing tax credit with new features, "bonus credits" as she describes them, to achieve outcomes in health, education, and household financial stability.[32] Or one could take this idea a step further beyond building real estate. What if the IRS created a new investment tax credit program and issued a Form 8609 for high school graduation?[33]

CDFIs are also able to create a suite of financing tools that could enable an outcomes-based financing system. One tool that CDFIs excel at is creating "capital stacks" that combine and braid together multiple sources of capital in a way that makes financing guardrail and airbag interventions much easier. These funds could also have outcomes tied to them. Maggie Super Church, of the Conservation Law Foundation, writes that a "creatively assembled capital stack of tax credit equity, multi-sector partnerships, and local support" can achieve complex social and health outcomes. One fund she helped cofound, the Healthy Neighborhood Equity Fund, tracks over fifty outcomes that the fund tries to improve in communities as a result of its investments. This technique of assembling multiple sources of capital and tying that investment to outcomes "can be replicated nearly anywhere. Individual and institutional investors, including banks, hospitals, and health systems, can bring new resources to the table, bolstered by first-loss capital from the public and philanthropic sectors," according to Super Church in her essay in *What Matters*.[34]

Innovative uses of capital tied to outcomes by CDFIs are not limited to creating capital stacks or funds. Nancy Andrews, former CEO of the Low Income Investment Fund, proposes a new financing product that she calls "Equity with a Twist," which enables community entrepreneurs (or "community quarterbacks" in her essay) using flexibility in their financing to achieve quick wins in social outcomes in addition to the other objectives of the fund, such as constructing affordable housing. "At the highest level, [it] is intended to demonstrate that integrative, outcomes-driven approaches can alleviate poverty."[35]

In a similar vein, Kimberlee Cornett describes the Kresge Foundation's Strong Families Fund, "a Kresge-led, multi-partner effort to fund up to 10 years of resident service coordination in Low Income Housing Tax Credit (LIHTC)–financed family housing through a

pay-for-performance, incentivized loan structure." For every social outcome achieved, the interest rate on the affordable housing mortgage is
reduced.[36]

The benefits that flow from outcomes-based funding are many, according to Brookings scholar Emily Gustafsson-Wright. Outcomes-
based financing "has enormous potential to help achieve equitable
access to quality social services. The greater focus on outcomes can
lead to flexibility, innovation, and adaptive learning in service delivery, and an emphasis on evaluation can enhance transparency in social spending and facilitate funding what works."[37] The flexibility and
real-time learning are critical to constant refinement and improvement. It is much better than the current model to pay someone to
follow a recipe that often does not work. Paying for outcomes creates
a demand that begins to reshape institutions, behaviors, relationships,
and culture. An open structure, like a market, will permit problem-
solving ideas to come from every direction. It is inherently antimo-
nopoly, pro-local, and community-empowering.

Bringing Buyers, Producers, and Connectors Together to Create a Market That Values Health?

To start, there need to be three actors to create a market: (1) buyers,
(2) producers or sellers, and (3) connectors who facilitate the transactions that allow buyers to pay producers for the desired outcome—
better health.[38] Chapter 4 is an in-depth discussion of how all these
ideas and components might land in one place to create the market
that values health. I hope in that thought experiment, the elements of
this marketplace will become easier to see. But before that case study,
consider this high-level explanation in broader brush strokes.

Buyers of health include the twin pillars already discussed in this
chapter: (1) spending on improving population health, and (2) Pay for
Success financing for social programs. In the health sector, there are
many entities willing to pay for better health, including Medicare,

Medicaid, the Veterans Administration, health insurers, integrated health care systems (both provider and payer, e.g., Kaiser Permanente), the growing number of accountable care-type organizations (ACOs and ACCs), and employers, particularly those that are self-insured. There are also buyers mentioned in the introduction (e.g., foundations, impact investors, and others targeting improved health as a goal). What they all have in common is that they all benefit from improved health of the overall population or their segment of the population.

The market does not work, however, unless there are producers of health. There are so many varied producers of health, but one way to summarize what most of them do is that they help people gain control over their own destiny, as described by Syme.[39] To recap, good schools, well-funded libraries, access to affordable housing, nutritious food, transportation, and jobs are all guardrail strategies that support good health. And the airbag strategies described previously—such as early childhood enrichment, mentors, and challenges in the realm of sports and arts—are also producers of health.

This market that values health does not overthrow old approaches to fighting poverty, rather, it incorporates them into a new whole. Strategies that exist today—Head Start, affordable housing, Meals on Wheels, job training, and the like—are all guardrail and airbag interventions that work to improve the social determinants of health. In other words, they are producers of health. This new market will both create more demand for that work and create greater accountability for success. And there are many ways to make these traditional programs simpler and easier to use, such as the automatic direct deposit of the expanded Child Tax Credit for low-income parents in the Biden administration's pandemic relief bill in 2021.[40]

The third bucket comprises those who connect the buyers to the producers. These "connectors" are often Pay for Success strategies as already discussed. They can be entities like a Real Estate Investment Trust (REIT). The Community Development Trust was started as an REIT in 1999 to connect investors to affordable housing investments.

Since then, they have provided over $2 billion to fund this critical upstream determinant of health using REITs and other financial vehicles.[41] Nico Echo Park is an innovative "neighborhood REIT" that allows residents to invest as little as $100 in their neighborhood's housing.[42] CDFIs are connectors that are capable of braiding multiple types of capital in a creative and patient way to fund affordable housing, social service organizations, charter schools, federal-qualified health clinics, and other guardrail and airbag investments. Examples we have already seen are the Healthy Neighborhood Equity Fund, the Low Income Investment Fund's Equity with a Twist Fund, and Kresge Foundation's Strong Families Fund.

Financing the Transition to the New Approach?

Most people would agree that we need to do a better job with our approach to antipoverty policy. They would also likely agree that we spend too much money on the wrong things in medical care, such as treating avoidable chronic disease. But unfortunately, you can't simply stop paying for those inefficiencies and transfer that money to a new upstream investment. You can't suddenly stop dialysis for a patient with kidney failure from Type 2 diabetes in order to fund an upstream intervention, such as a grocery store in a food desert. The current train full of avoidable chronic disease is already hurtling down the tracks, and it is hard to imagine how we can simply pick it up and put it on a new and better track focused on prevention. How do we make the switch?

Part of the answer is that we will have to use private-sector resources to start this process. Social impact bonds and other Pay for Success vehicles will attract investors with a financial return from cost savings. Other new-track money will include investments from foundations, pension funds, and other investors looking for social impact. Universities and health care systems fulfilling their role as anchor institutions in communities can play a part.[43] Recently fourteen of the largest health care systems in the country, all part of the Healthcare Anchor Network, pledged $700 million toward efforts to address the upstream drivers behind widening health disparities.[44] And in January 2021 the Office of the Surgeon General released a report titled, *Community Health and Economic Prosperity: Engaging Businesses as Stewards and Stakeholders*, focused on the important role of the private business sector investing in communities to both improve important upstream determinants of health and to improve their own bottom line.[45]

And finally, when you have an entity that is on the hook for downstream medical care costs, it motivates them to think upstream. It becomes easier to use dollars in the medical field to pay for preschool or affordable housing, which has been happening in pockets all over the country for years. In addition to the ACOs, Managed Care Organizations (MCOs), ACHs, and ACCs discussed earlier, there is significant innovation on this front with programs like Centers for Medicare and Medicaid Innovation, State Innovation Models (SIM) initiative,[46] and the Collaborative Approach to Public Good Investments model.[47] A similar concept of how you might create the right incentives to invest at the individual level was proposed by Rebecca Nielsen, David Muhlestein, and Michael Leavitt in their Health Affairs blog *Forefront*, "Social Determinants of Health: Aggregated Precision Investment."[48] All these strategies are promising solutions to the "wrong pocket problem," where the economic benefits of an intervention (e.g., avoided chronic disease) flow to the health insurer and not organizations that built the park and grocery store in a food desert. And another promising model that focuses on a place, like Maui, is the experiment known as the Geographic Direct Contracting Model from CMS.[49] That approach is more focused on coordinated medical care, but it could be a good model for alignment and upstream investing for social determinants as well.

Tying all this together will be linked payments from outcomes-based financing and redirected medical care dollars spent on the upstream social determinants. There is a lot more thinking needed in the outcomes area, but you can imagine that it would include more babies born healthy into homes ready to accept them, more students reading at grade level, managing allostatic load among stressed populations, and improved self-reported health (a surprisingly accurate assessment of actual health).[50]

How the Pieces Fit Together in a Place—Pilots

In order to work out the details of how this new approach will work, we will need to experiment in smaller places where some entity (an insurance company, a large employer, the government) owns the majority of the downstream medical-care cost risk. In these pockets, the incentives for the health sector will be aligned with the existing incentives of the antipoverty and community development sectors. In other words, the buyers of health will be easier to organize to make investments to support upstream determinants of health.

These places will also need to have sufficient numbers of producers of health. I think all places have these producers and all places can build capacity in this area, but to start, we need a strong network of health producers who can effectively provide guardrails and airbags for a community. We will need the advantage of this leg up to prove the concept that we can, in a place, make sure that every person struggling—from substance abuse, mental illness, or the challenges of aging without help, and other challenges—has the support they need.

Connectors are a bit easier to import, so in this case, we could bring in CDFIs, impact investors, bankers, and other connectors to help connect the buyers to the producers.

As the market that values health grows, it will attract innovators. It would be exciting to see the enormous problem-solving capacity of Silicon Valley, for example, focus on developing the full potential of vulnerable children rather than faster ways to deliver a package or share cat videos. As an example, Neighborly.com was an online municipal bond broker dealer that experimented with a "Ready to Learn at Kindergarten" bond that would allow impact investors and other "buyers" of health to finance a panoply of services for children to engage their growing brains in early childhood.

Another critical type of connector will be those that help manage information and data. This is a need at every scale—individual to family to neighborhood to region. When someone has overlapping needs from multiple service providers, the complexity can be overwhelming. An example is the work of Unite US providing coordinated and aligned support to veterans. Santa Clara County, California (home of Silicon Valley), is also making some breakthroughs in this area for their homeless population. Santa Clara County's Project Welcome Home is a partnership with the software company Palantir to create an integrated data platform to coordinate and track interventions with the county's homeless population. "The platform has integrated key datasets from different departments in the County to triage and identify the highest need utilizers in the County's systems, conduct outreach and enrollment in the program and monitor and track client's progress in the permanent supportive housing program," according to the county's website.[51]

All this new train track building will require breakthroughs in technology to align, coordinate, and respond to changing needs. I have touched on this topic already, but you can imagine technology platforms like the one Palantir built for Santa Clara County being a technology backbone to the new approach. That system keeps close ties to each homeless person in the county, tracks their use of social services, and helps align responses to get the best outcome for those individuals. The service coordinator, Unite US, does something similar with its platform to treat the social, medical, and mental health needs of veterans and other patient groups.

How you coordinate this massive amount of data using blockchain technology may be especially promising since it allows for protection of privacy while simultaneously allowing multiple service providers to go into and out of a person's case history. Artificial intelligence and machine learning can also play a role, like when someone misses a dentist appointment, to coordinate a response (some "fellowship") at critical junctures in a person's life. It can also help with many of the known challenges of transitioning from one stage of life to the next (e.g., childhood to adolescence), where we know extra airbags might be a wise investment.

New organizational structures will be part of the new track. Clusters of organizations would develop specialties and coordinate around areas of practice. Some of those clusters might focus around unleashing the creativity of children and community members through the arts or the sense of connection and discipline one gets from sports. Others could organize around stage of life—childhood, adolescence, young adulthood. Still others on creating prepared workers with job training and first jobs as in the REDF model (which provides wraparound social supports and guaranteed employment in worker-friendly businesses they own). Some clusters will focus more on places and specialize in building out the needs of lifelong learning—schools, museums, libraries. Others could focus on transportation and affordable housing

In this marketplace, there will be community entrepreneurs who will innovate to provide new approaches and strategies to achieve the outcomes called for in the Pay for Success funding programs. These entrepreneurs will need data and analysis. They will need partners who can deliver on certain aspects of an outcomes-oriented business plan. Consider the analogy of a contractor building a house. A contractor has to coordinate subcontractors, such as the carpenter, plumber, electrician, and painter. Similarly, the community entrepreneur will have to assemble a team of "social subcontractors"—teachers, affordable-housing builders, household financial stability coaches, nurses—to meet the needs of the community.

This combination of contractors and subcontractors will be different in every place; no one size fits all. This is why policies and programs emanating from Washington, DC, or state capitals, fail so often. In some places, issues around racial justice and healing might be the first priority. In other places, the highest-order concerns may have more to do with a deadly scourge of opioid addiction, requiring a public health intervention to stabilize the community. A third community might be struggling with the loss of low-skill / middle-wage jobs at a factory, mill, or rural regional hospital. In this third case, the first intervention might be to focus on the stability of families in economic transition (especially their children), with a tighter focus on job retraining and optional relocation to higher-opportunity communities. Still other interventions might first focus on the celebration of local culture—newly arrived Micronesians to Hawaii or Mexican Americans in the Colonias along the Texas border, for instance—as a first building block toward building stronger community cohesion and a foundation on which to brainstorm plans to lift the community. All communities have different assets and challenges; therefore, all health-promoting interventions will be different and tailor-made.

In all cases, the community entrepreneurs will have to use their knowledge of the community to guide their strategies. Of course, that strategy will constantly be challenged or reinforced by using real-time data to measure progress. Hitting the appropriate milestones along the path to the ultimate outcome will be critical. And the strategy will have to evolve constantly. What worked in the first time period will not work in subsequent time periods. Solving one problem (e.g., crime) often triggers another problem that will require new types of interventions (e.g., gentrification and displacement).

Benefits of the Market That Values Health

The market that values health is designed to help vulnerable people thrive. The recipients of the intervention described here are likely to be concentrated in low-income communities, but they could be living in high-income communities too. In the past, we have concentrated our efforts on low-income people in low-income neighborhoods. There were good reasons to do this because these were the areas of highest need. It allowed for better coordination of services. But a new mechanism could cast a wider net to identify those in need who are living in middle-income or even affluent geographies. The concentrations would be less (5 to 10 percent of the residents, perhaps), but the total opportunity may be greater because there are more of those communities (what epidemiologists refer to as population attributable risk).[52] This wider net could apply the same market for better social outcomes as will exist in low-income areas. In addition to helping more people, this universal aspect of the approach can build wider political support in a way that we also see for Social Security or Medicare. It also achieves the goals outlined by jon powell [lower case by request] and his Berkeley colleagues in the concept of "targeted universalism." Targeted universalism "means setting universal goals pursued by targeted processes to achieve those goals," according to powell and his coauthors, a concept that clearly resonates with the market that values health.[53]

Expanding this market to cover wider geographies also solves a problem identified by Elizabeth Kneebone and Emily Garr, where they found that "by 2008, suburbs were home to the largest and fastest-growing poor population in the country."[54] The market that values health would be a new tool to reach into those areas with little history of poverty, and thus fewer institutions to address it. The market would help organize social service networks that do not have the benefit of long-standing relationships and geographic density, as exist in older urban centers.

This new market will create new job ladders for community entrepreneurs and their social subcontractors in their communities. We saw something like this happen in community development, where local residents in low-income communities got their first jobs at the neighborhood CDC. Over time, they developed skills and contacts that were valuable to other employers, and many went into government or the private sector. This created a new job ladder in communities that had fewer connections to gain experience and advance professionally.

More than anything, however, the market that values health will create a dynamic response to an ever-changing problem of providing the social support to ensure that all people thrive.

Risks of the Market That Values Health

I recognize that this approach to financing social change has risks. It will be disruptive and will create winners and losers. Many organizations that have long track records of helping communities might not be able to successfully compete in this new outcomes marketplace. We must anticipate the need for legacy organizations to transition to new funding realities or find compassionate ways to wind them down. Antony Bugg-Levine, former CEO of Nonprofit Finance Fund, cautions us, "Realizing this potential [of outcomes-based financing] will require all of us to honestly acknowledge how many of our cherished practices and assumptions are accommodations to a broken system rather than necessary or beneficial."[55]

For good reason, the composition of interventions (especially airbags) will change over time. Current investments that cater to the consequences of living in poverty, such as prisons, or dialysis centers in places with high rates of diabetes, would close. This adjustment would not happen overnight, but in the future, there will be more preschool teachers and reading tutors and fewer prison guards and nephrologists. We do not want to make the same mistake of letting communities fend for themselves during deindustrialization, outsourcing of jobs, and other structural job losses triggered by technological change. Finding compassionate ways to make this transition will be important.

Many early critics of the quasi-market for community development—the use of block grants and tax credits rather than direct government expenditures—argued that it was overly complicated. The question was, why should we create a convoluted system that rewards too many lawyers and accountants just to structure complicated financing deals aimed at helping low-income people? But as anyone who had an organization languish under the earlier regime dominated by erratic direct funding decisions from Washington bureaucracies would attest, the new system, although complicated, was better.[56]

Some critics also say that getting the interventions right is too complicated. Understanding what allows people to thrive, what gives them hope, the dynamics of a neighborhood, or the complex adaptive problem of poverty requires a level of research and analysis that goes beyond our current capabilities. Of course, this may be true, but as Jack Shonkoff said at a Federal Reserve System Community Development Research Conference, "Cancer is complicated. Because something is complicated is not an excuse for not tackling the problem."[57]

Other critics, particularly those who are more politically liberal, associate the market with sweatshops and economic exploitation. Economist Dean Baker has argued that it does not make sense to see the market itself as "the enemy" just because it has been used in nefarious ways: "This makes as much sense as seeing the wheel as the enemy. The market is a tool, it is incredibly malleable."[58]

However, while markets have great ability to allocate resources efficiently, they do not always do so fairly. As with all markets, this one will need diligent regulation and monitoring to guard against dynamics that might commodify social service interventions and create perverse incentives for payouts. For a thoughtful distributive-justice critique of outcomes-based financing, see Jodi Halpern and Doug Jutte's essay, "The Ethics of Outcomes-Based Funding Models," in *What Matters*.[59] "Adhering to outcomes metrics isn't enough," they write. "The moral and ethical implications of how those metrics are defined and delivered should be part of the conversation as well."

Conclusion

How a community wields that market power on its own behalf is an opportunity to bring a sense of control for an entire community. It is a means of wielding power locally. In my book, *Housing Policy Revolution*, I write about how community activists were eager to embrace the current approach to community development finance because it gave them the power over local market-related decisions rather than depending on the decisions of distant bureaucrats.[60] The market can be radically liberating with the appropriate constraints. Abraham Lincoln had this flash of insight as a boy. He was born poor, to an abusive father, but he found liberation as a kid operating a raft on the Mississippi. He got paid $2 to ferry workers from the shore to the waiting riverboats. His labor was a source of income and independence.[61] Similarly, the market can be a tool for local control and community agency.

Buyers, producers, and connectors will operate this marketplace against a backdrop, or ecosystem, which must have a number of elements in order to be successful. The most critical is that the people who are served by this market believe it is in their best interest to engage in it. Low-income and struggling communities are too familiar with eager foundation or government staff who propose potential solutions to their problems—the new shiny object—but lose interest over time when success is elusive. That cycle of excitement, frustration, and then abandonment has been experienced many times by low-income communities all across the country. If the market that values health is to succeed, it will require a sustained commitment and champions within the low-income community that is the focus of the upstream intervention.

CHAPTER 4

Hawaii Case Study

How an Island State Can Point the Way

BREAKING THE "CAKE OF CUSTOM," as Walter Bagehot wrote in *Physics and Politics* in 1872, often happens first in a smaller place and then radiates outward. Adam Smith described how the modern economy did this when it first took root in semiautonomous Northern European cities in the late 1400s and early 1500s. These cities were granted special legal charters to operate their society and economy in new ways that allowed something that began to resemble organized labor (guilds) and investment capital (proto-banks) to create local economies that looked very modern. The changes in organizing labor and capital unleashed tremendous productive power in these places, and not surprisingly, new sources of economic and political power. Smith questions why the feudal lords would be willing to bargain away their power over these cities. (It is extremely rare in human history for those with power to give it up!) He concluded that it was in pursuit of luxuries, "diamond buckles perhaps," that the lords "gradually bartered their whole power and authority."[1] Smith described these newly thriving city economies as "islands in a feudal sea."

How labor and capital were organized changed over time, grew more sophisticated, and created explosive economic growth. The growth brought wealth, innovation, and power to city leaders. Soon that power began to extend beyond the city walls and rival the authority of the traditional rulers. In time, the modern economy would take over the countryside, the emerging nation-states, and the world.

I believe that using outcomes-based financing and population-health business models that focus on improving the upstream social determinants of health will create markets-that-value-health islands in a sea of systems designed to treat avoidable disease with expensive medical care. This will happen first in the places that have a special combination of factors and characteristics that make this transformation more likely. Those places will have buyers and producers of health as well as the entities to connect them (as described in the introduction and chapter 3). Similar to the way that the modern economy took root in Northern European cities, these markets-that-value-health geographies will lead a transformation in how we provide social services upstream to avoid expenses downstream. There are many areas that have characteristics favorable to this change in approach, and in this chapter I focus on one—Hawaii.

Why Hawaii?

There are many places in the United States that have the right combination of buyers, producers, and connectors to jumpstart the market that values health. I have been fortunate in my role working in the community development function of the Federal Reserve System for the last seventeen years to visit many of them, some of which I'm describing here:

Lincoln, Nebraska, has a progressive health conversion foundation, good local government, and many capable nonprofits to produce health.

Denver has a forward-thinking medical community, innovative housing authority, and the resources of the very well-endowed Colorado Health Foundation.

Salt Lake City has been on the forefront of Pay for Success financing experiments and also has the innovative integrated health system Intermountain Health.

Columbus, Ohio, through the leadership of Nationwide Children's Hospital, has an extensive Accountable Care Organization program for children in the Columbus area and southeastern Ohio that has been successful in a value-based approach to children's health.[2]

North Carolina state government has been very innovative in its health policies, especially with its Centers for Medicare & Medicare Services–approved waiver that allows it to use $650 million in Medicaid dollars to pay for nonmedical needs, including housing, transportation, food, and interpersonal violence and toxic stress.[3] And the majority of the citizens of that state are insured by one health insurer, Blue Cross Blue Shield of North Carolina.[4]

Massachusetts is the pioneer in global budgeting for medical care, which aligns many of the buyers of health.

Many rural counties in the United States (especially in Medicaid expansion states) where there is only one health insurance company, are the very definition of "owning" the downstream medical care cost risk.

And finally, it might also be possible to focus on the special needs of a segment of the population rather than a geography—veterans, Native Americans, or the groundbreaking work of CityBlock Health in Manhattan—that has a population-health business model which was forged in treating the communities ravaged by the HIV/AIDS epidemic.[5]

But, to me, the one place that stood out from this list was the island of Maui in Hawaii. Almost half the residents of Maui are insured by Kaiser Permanente. And thanks to a merger, Kaiser now operates all three hospitals on the island as well. When you have most of the population as policyholders (often for their lifetimes) and you operate the hospitals, which means you are on the hook for readmission costs for vulnerable patients like those who are homeless, then you have an entity that starts thinking as a buyer of upstream health. And as I learned more about the circumstances on other Hawaiian Islands, it became clear to me that beyond just Maui, the entire state of Hawaii is poised to be the place where we could break the cake of custom and create a population health business model in a fee-for-service sea.

The state of Hawaii evokes images of a tropical paradise, and although it is beautiful, it has not avoided the social, economic, and environmental problems that afflict other parts of the United States. At the same time, it has many advantages to promote health—especially for vulnerable people. Although many have suggested that using Hawaii as the example for the market that values health is a mistake because it is so different from most other parts of the country, it is a good case study for a number of reasons. First, it is racially diverse. White Alone (in the language of the U.S. Census) count for just 25.5 percent of the population. Native Hawaiians are 10 percent. Two or more races are 24.2 percent. While the percentage of Black (2.2 percent) and Hispanics (10.7 percent) are proportionally smaller than in the continental United States, Asian Alone is the largest plurality in the state at 37.6 percent, according to the 2019 U.S. Census.[6] Second, it had about the national average per capita personal income in 2019 at just over $57,000[7] and a similar rate of poverty (9.5 percent versus 10.5 percent). Third, life expectancy varies dramatically over short distances as it does in other areas of the United States (see figure 4.1).[8]

And finally, given the following health and upstream challenges Hawaii faces outlined following here, I would argue that Hawaii is more similar to other communities across the country than people realize.

FIGURE 4.1

Life Expectancy At Birth, Years
by Tract, CDC and NCHS 2010–15
- Over 87 Years
- 84–87 Years
- 81–84 Years
- 78–81 Years
- 75–78 Years
- 72–75 Years
- 72 Years or Less
- No Data or Data Suppressed

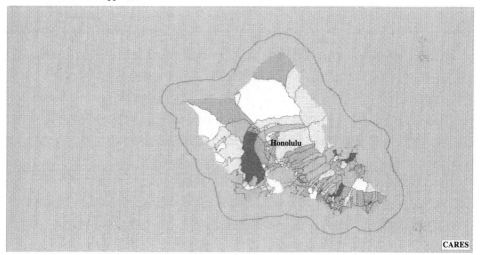

Challenges to Health in Hawaii

Like many places in the United States, Hawaii has had to shift from an agriculture-based economy to a service-based economy. Hawaiian agriculture was a vibrant economic sector from the nineteenth century to the 1970s, when falling transportation costs and new competition for tropical agriculture grew more intense with production from low-wage countries in Asia and the Caribbean. In this way, the Hawaiian economy looks similar to other plantation economies forced to transition away from historical production, such as the decline of cotton agriculture in the American South. And it is not too far from the experience of shifting economic fortunes of other single-sector manufacturing cities like those dependent on textiles in New England or steel producers and other heavy manufacturing in the Midwest.

Fortunately for Hawaii, the falling transportation cost that so damaged the agricultural economy was a boon to the tourist industry. But the transition to an economy based on tourism has not always created enough economic opportunity for all residents of the state. Wages tend to be low in that sector, and Hawaii has notoriously high costs of living. The average hourly wage in Honolulu, for example, appears high at over $25 per hour. But an analysis by *Governing* magazine that factored in cost of living put the cost-adjusted hourly wage as the second-lowest in the country at about $15 per hour.[9] This phenomenon of middle wages and high costs is part of the explanation for why 42 percent of households were struggling to make ends meet; a little more than 9 percent were under the federal poverty line, and another 33 percent were Asset-Limited, Income-Constrained, Employed, or ALICE, according to a study by the United Way of Hawaii.[10]

This same dynamic clouds how one understands poverty in Hawaii as well. The traditional measure of poverty in use since the 1960s ignores variations in cost of living across the country. By that measure, Hawaii's 9.5 percent living below the official poverty threshold is below the national average of 10.5 percent.[11] But the cost of living in Honolulu can be even more expensive than living in San Francisco or New York without the higher wages of those cities.[12] A more accurate assessment of the circumstances on the ground uses the Census Bureau's Supplemental Poverty Measure (SPM), which considers both the cost of living and government assistance. By that measure, Hawaii has 13.7 percent living below the SPM, which is the thirteenth highest rate in the United States.[13]

Housing is a challenge in Hawaii as it is in most states. The National Low Income Housing Coalition does an annual survey of the hourly wage necessary to rent a two-bedroom home by state, and in 2020, Hawaii had the highest housing wage in the country at $38.76.

In Hawaii, the fair market rent for a two-bedroom apartment is $2,015. "In order to afford this level of rent and utilities—without paying more than 30% of income on housing—a household must earn $6,718 monthly or $80,613 annually," according to the Coalition's report "Out of Reach." With 42 percent of households renting, housing is a cost burden on nearly all but the highest-earning families.[14] Given this high cost relative to local wages and mild weather, it is no surprise that Hawaii also has one of the highest percentages of homelessness in the country. Hawaii ranks fourth among all states, with 45 people per 100,000 being homeless in 2019.[15]

It may be hard to imagine that a former agricultural powerhouse would have such a significant problem with hunger, but nearly one in eight people experience food insecurity in Hawaii.[16] Food insecurity is defined as households unable to provide adequate food for one or more household members due to lack of resources. Food insecurity causes a number of health problems. A study by the Centers for Disease Control and Prevention estimates that hunger cost Hawaii $183 million in 2019.[17] According to that study, this cost was driven by poor health outcomes caused by "worse dietary quality in food-insecure individuals; trade-offs between food and other basics, such as medications, that make chronic disease management more difficult; and psychological factors, including stress and depressive symptoms."[18] It is worth pausing here—better food security for Hawaii could save the health system tens of millions of dollars in just one year. This is a great example of how solving an upstream problem creates downstream savings.

Comparatively speaking, Hawaii is a healthy state. But like others, it is struggling with some very concerning health issues, including the following:

Diabetes has increased in prevalence by 35 percent between 2012 and 2019 from 7.8 percent to 10.5 percent of adults.[19]

The youth suicide rate doubled between 2007 and 2011; it is the leading cause of death for those aged 15 to 24.[20]

Only 19 percent of adults were obese in 1997, but that percentage rose to 24 percent in 2017.[21]

Drug overdoses are on the rise and outnumber traffic-related deaths; the average drug overdose rate doubled from the 1999–2003 time period to the 2010–2014 period.[22]

These overlapping economic, housing, health, and other challenges require a coordinated response, according to the Hawai'i Appleseed Center for Law and Economic Justice. In their 2016 report, "State of Poverty in Hawai'i," they sounded the alarm that progress against the many problems facing Hawaii requires a much bigger and better coordinated effort. "Elected officials, the business community, policymakers, and the broader community must come together and recognize that many of the most pressing problems in our community—homelessness, lack of educational achievement, obesity and chronic illnesses—are closely linked with a lack of income that leaves struggling families unable to meet their basic needs, pushing them over the edge."[23] Hawaii, like many places in the United States, needs more guardrails and airbags. Fortunately, it has many of the institutions and community-based organizations to provide them as well as many buyers of health that might be in a position to pay for them.

Hawaii's Many Advantages to Improve Upstream Determinants of Health

Although there are many challenges in Hawaii, the state also has many assets and advantages that create a favorable environment for the market that values health. Geography is one. The islands help minimize the "churn" of people in and out of a specific geography that you see in the continental United States, where moving between states or regions is relatively easy or where populated metro areas cross state lines. This is important as we try to isolate which upstream interventions and approaches are most effective. And because health insurers in Hawaii, for example, often have a relationship with a policyholder for a lifetime, upstream investments in guardrails—such as high-quality schools—start to make sense financially because they generate savings downstream on medical care costs. This fact goes a long way to solving the "wrong pocket problem," where the entity paying for upstream interventions cannot recoup that investment because the benefit flows to another entity.

Local government in the state can be a leader in pulling together the necessary parties because it is not as fragmented as in other parts of the country. For example, each of the islands is also a county (Maui County also includes the islands of Molokai and Lanai). Each island has a single mayor and county council. Also, unexpectedly, the entire state has only one school district and a single housing authority. As I have witnessed myself, it is possible to gather the leaders of all these sectors around a single table, which greatly simplifies the conversation about creating new health-promoting programs across those systems.

The fact that each island is a county has another advantage. In the United States, most of the health and wellbeing data that could guide a market that values health effort is collected at the county level. Having county-level data in Los Angeles County is meaningless since it is impossible to tease out any insights for what is happening in terms of cause and effect for its ten million residents across dozens of cities, towns, and unincorporated areas. And Atlanta sits atop three to seven counties, depending on how one defines the city/metro area.[24] Identifying cause-and-effect relationships is easier with Maui County's 167,000 residents, especially since we know the population is the same, more or less, over time.[25] In essence, this characteristic means there is a built-in and free "pre/post" evaluation of the market that values health.

In spite of its middle-of-the-pack per capita income, Hawaii has pockets of extreme wealth; it has the fourth highest number of millionaires in the United States.[26] This has contributed to the rise of a vibrant philanthropic and socially motivated investing sector. For a population of only 1.4 million, Hawaii has 487 private foundations, according to data compiled by the Urban Institute's National Center of Charitable Statistics.[27] And the Kamehameha Schools foundation (dedicated to educating Native Hawaiians) is ranked as the eleventh wealthiest foundation in the world with an endowment over $11 billion.[28]

As diverse as the population is in the state of Hawaii, there is shared respect from all groups of Native Hawaiian culture, which serves as a bridge to those diverse groups. I want to be clear that my intent here is not to be disrespectful to a group that has suffered from discrimination. But there are concepts in Hawaiian culture that might serve as a lattice on which to build the market that values health. For example, *kuleana* is the Hawaiian word that is often translated into English as *responsibility*. But it means more than that. There is a sense of reciprocity embedded in kuleana. An example often cited is that the people have a responsibility to care for the land and their environment. The land, in return, has a responsibility to feed, clothe, and shelter the people.[29] It is very common in gatherings in the state of Hawaii for people with very different ancestry (e.g., from Asia, Africa, Pacific Islands, or Europe) and across sectors (e.g., banking, housing, health care, government) to use words like *kuleana*, *pono* (righteousness), *mahalo* (thanks, gratitude, admiration, praise), and *aina* (land/that which feeds) when they are arguing how to improve public policies. These words—and the Native Hawaiian culture behind them—can serve as inspiration as we reimagine how we can create a new social welfare system to better care for all our fellow citizens.

Buyers, Producers, and Connectors in Hawaii

The key to creating a market that values health is to reorganize buyers, producers, and connectors in a way that is economically sustainable. Buyers are in the position to create demand for this market because they "own" the downstream medical care cost risk for a certain population. And in the instances where this responsibility lasts a long time, they recognize the importance of investing early in the upstream social determinants of health as a strategy to save on future, downstream medical care expenses. In many places in the United States, there are too many buyers. Organizing this atomized group is an overwhelming task. But in Hawaii, there are fewer buyers, and they are more likely to join together.

In Hawaii, there are two health insurers who dominate the market: 1) HMSA has more than 50 percent of Hawaiian residents as policy holders; and 2) Kaiser Permanente has about 20 percent of residents and operates all three hospitals and many clinics on Maui. Medicaid and Medicare insure about 45 percent of Hawaiian residents. Other large insurers include Hawaii Management Alliance Association, University Health Alliance, Aloha Care, UnitedHealthcare, Humana, and Centene with the remaining 30 percent of the health insurance market.[30]

Hawaii also has only a handful of large employers. The U.S. military is a sizable one, along with some of the larger hospitality/travel companies. As in most places, the hospital systems are very large employers. And a few big players, such as the Bank of Hawaii and others, have sizable concentrations of employees in pockets around the state and could be brought in as buyers of health.

The state of Hawaii's Department of Human Services (DHS) is a particularly interesting buyer of health—especially with its Ohana Nui Medicaid project. This program, spearheaded by a previous DHS director, Rachael Wong, is designed to improve the health of both families and communities. *Ohana* is the Hawaiian word for family, and *nui* is translated as big—so this has a rough translation as extended family. The name was chosen by young adults who had been part of DHS's foster child system. "The name can be seen as a reflection of our culture and a way to honor the extended families, including aunts and uncles, coaches, teachers, spiritual advisers, and many others not necessarily related by blood, but who are nevertheless considered 'ohana,'" according to the DHS report. The areas of focus for Ohana Nui are housing/shelter, food/nutrition, health/wellness, education/economic support, and social capital.

Ohana Nui is a two-generation strategy with a focus on children, according to a DHS report on the history of the program. One manifestation of this focus is the effort to reduce adverse childhood experiences, or ACEs, as a way to avoid lifetime costs to treat emotional and health needs caused by those experiences.[31]

Putting the family at the center is a strategy to rethink how services are delivered by both the Department of Human Services and the Department of Health. Dr. Virginia Pressler, former director of the Department of Health, wants to see more coordination between the two government agencies. "We have many of the same providers that DHS has. We see the same patients," she observed. "We are specifically looking into how we can legally share data between our programs and our departments. The focus is to look at an entire family unit and its dynamics."[32]

This nod to design thinking, where the experience of the end user—the family—is at the center of the intervention, is not easy. "To accomplish this overall goal it is necessary to align state programs and funding around a common framework: a multigenerational, culturally appropriate approach that invests in children and families over the life-cycle to nurture well-being and improve individual and population health outcomes," according to Judy Mohr Peterson, a researcher of the program's effectiveness.[33] "This intentional disruption of a decades-long approach to human services delivery is the key to giving individuals and families the best chance at creating a cycle of intergenerational opportunity," according to Kimberly Miyazawa Frank, the DHS director of Community Development.[34]

Hospital operators are also owners of downstream medical care cost risk, in part because of the Affordable Care Act provisions that put medical care providers on the hook when a patient is readmitted to the hospital for the same malady. If a patient returns with the same medical problem within thirty days, Medicare will not reimburse the hospital for the subsequent visit. This puts pressure on health care systems to better understand the environment and conditions into which they are discharging their patients and to take steps to ensure that those conditions do not put the patient at risk of falling ill again shortly after successful treatment. If a patient is homeless, for example, exposure to the elements might exacerbate pulmonary illness, then the hospital is incentivized to find a way to house the patient. It might also incentivize a hospital—as a buyer of health—to make investments to speed the construction of affordable housing that "produces" health. While a hospital's charitable giving—"community benefit" in health care lingo—can play a role, so too can direct investments from the hospital's "treasury" or investment portfolio.

There are many nonmedical sources of capital in the buyer category as well. Traditional community development finance is one, especially banks motivated by the Community Reinvestment Act (CRA). The banks in Hawaii are particularly good partners in the market that values health because, unlike other parts of the country, all the banks in Hawaii are headquartered in that state. Most Americans are customers with one of the five big commercial banks, which are headquartered in faraway New York, Charlotte, or San Francisco. But the banks based in the state of Hawaii know local needs and, importantly, are required to make their CRA investments locally.

There are funds from traditional government sources, such as the Community Development Block Grant, HOME Investment Partnership, Healthy Foods Financing Initiative, and the investment tax credits (New Markets and the Low-Income Housing Tax Credit). In addition to these hundreds of millions of dollars flowing to Hawaii every year, there are new programs, such as the funds motivated by Opportunity Zones, which was part of the Tax Cuts and Jobs Act of 2017.[35]

The small number of buyers—insurers, the military, the tourism industry, hospital systems, and a few other large employers—makes Hawaii an ideal place to focus on how those entities could be organized to get better long-term outcomes in health. Add to this the sizable resources available to improve the upstream social determinants of health from many foundations and socially minded wealthy investors, and you have the demand side of the equations—the buyers—to create a market that values health.

There Are Many Capable Producers of Health to Build Guardrails and Install Airbags

As explained earlier, guardrails are the type of neighborhood or community characteristics that provide some needed amenity or service that can enhance opportunities and increase the likelihood of living to one's potential. Guardrails include affordable housing, living-wage jobs, high-quality schools and libraries, adequate transportation, and so on.

Hawaii is fortunate that it has a relatively strong local economy that creates jobs and an economic floor for most families—even though many of them struggle with the high cost of living there. Providing support for families so they can move beyond the struggling circumstances described in the United Way's ALICE report is an essential foundation for improving health in Hawaii. There are access-to-jobs guardrails here, but they need to be strengthened.

Hawaii has many social programs to promote health and well-being, especially for children (often referred to by the Hawaiian word *keiki*). One innovative program that "puts the baby in the center of table," as Marian Wright Edelman famously counsels, is the organization Early Childhood Action Strategy (ECAS). ECAS "brings together diverse stakeholders, including government and nongovernment organizations, to improve the system of care for Hawai'i's youngest keiki," according to their website. Below is an organizational chart that shows the comprehensive nature that this organization's approach, achieved in coalition with its many partners, to implementing system-level interventions that create a nurturing ecosystem that achieves measurable goals, such as arriving at kindergarten ready to learn.[36] This approach is the very essence of an upstream strategy to improve health (see figure 4.2).

The list of partners is long and includes the state's Department of Health mentioned above and many other state agencies (Education,

FIGURE 4.2 Early Childhood Action Strategy Org Chart and Network Structure[36]

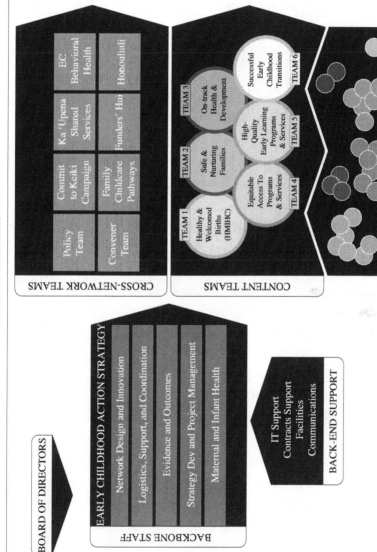

ECAS Network Structure

Human Services, Child Welfare Services), the United Way, the American Academy of Pediatrics, Big Brothers Big Sisters, YMCA, Campaign for Grade Level Reading, Hawai'i State Coalition Against Domestic Violence, Hawai'i Appleseed (authors of the poverty report mentioned earlier), and connector/funders, such as the Hawai'i Community Foundation and Kamehameha Schools, colleges and universities, and many others. All these organizations are guided by a robust data effort that measures progress toward achievable and measurable outcomes, including the following:

More babies are born healthy.
More children develop on-track.
More children enter kindergarten school-ready.
More children are proficient learners by third grade.

ECAS is a great example of a data-driven, systems-level intervention attempting to provide the guardrails and airbags for keiki so they arrive into adulthood with the skills and preparation they need to thrive. The focus on data is a particularly strong aspect of this strategy and is related to another Hawaiian organization, a tech startup called Kumu, which is attempting to use data to map other interventions to achieve system-level improvements.

Kumu is a tech startup in Hawaii that is seeking to marry technology to the tackling of complex adaptive systems work. "Whether you call them wicked, complex, intractable, or just plain broken, our society is facing many tough issues. We can't sit back and hope for the best. It's up to us to work through the complexity and create thoughtful, sustainable solutions," according to the company's website. The Waianae Alliance—a community group based on the Waianae coast of southwestern Oahu—used this tool to map the ecosystem that influenced child outcomes in their community. They were motivated to know the answer to this question: What factors contribute to the health and wellness of children in Waianae (positive and negative) and how are these factors interrelated? In this analysis, the Alliance identified two areas where they thought they might have leverage to improve child outcomes: (1) connection to the land and its connection to farming and healthy eating, and (2) adult and near-peer role models to help set positive examples to emulate.[38] Seeing a complex map of all the negative and positive influences on a child is also a powerful way to think about what guardrails and airbags are missing, or need to be strengthened, in a community.

This concept of human connection to the land combined with approaches to farming and healthy eating is an important guardrail to improve health. And as many words as I used in English to describe that idea, it is much more efficiently and elegantly captured in the Hawaiian word *aina*. There are some really groundbreaking interventions for kids in this sector. One of them is the Ma'O Organic Farms, where their motto is "Growing Food, Growing Leaders." Their mission is to build "a future of mā'ona, of plenty, by connecting youth and land through the daily practice of aloha 'āina, empowering youth to succeed in college and secure sustaining careers, and growing organic produce that yields individual and communal vitality."[39] In essence, Ma'O Farms is an organization that operates organic farms to provide sustainable and healthy foods and an education and job training program. To describe it in these terms, however, leaves out the many ripples of hope that radiate from this organization. Ma'O doesn't just grow food, it changes lives. And not just the lives of those who participate in the program. Research from the University of Hawaii shows that even those people who are part of the social network of Ma'O interns experienced measurable improvements in health and wellbeing, including a reduction in A1C levels (blood sugar levels, a diabetes predictor). The study analyzed body mass index, A1C, and gut microbiome composition. The University of Hawaii researchers, Alika Maunakea (a medical doctor) and Ruben Juarez (an economist), monitored interns at the farm from the baseline numbers to a one-year follow-up and found that those who were considered to be pre-diabetic had dropped by 30 percent. What was even more amazing was the influence those interns had on improving the health behaviors, such as healthier eating, for other young people in the interns' social networks.[40]

Using aina as a strategy to improve health and create connectedness to traditional Hawaiian foods and traditions has also been embraced by the state of Hawaii school system's lunch program in an effort called 'Aina Pono. "The Hawaii State Department of Education is increasing local food in student meals as well as connecting our keiki (children) with the 'āina (land) through their food, using products from the local agricultural community," according to the Department's website.[41] The change was not easy, according to Mililani High School cafeteria manager Debora Kam: "We were all used to simply unpacking or unwrapping processed foods like breaded chicken patties or nuggets, working in different stages by ourselves. With 'Aina Pono, everyone had to come together and collaborate to cut fruits or cook meals. It required all of our staff to work as a team and communicate with one another." But the effort paid off. The number of kids participating in the school lunch program doubled in a year. "It's just like going back to the old days," said Kam. "We have many mothers in our cafeteria staff, and if you love the kids, cooking from scratch and featuring local ingredients is what we have to do. We do it for our kids because we know that this way of cooking is healthier."

And this program isn't just benefiting kids; by focusing on buying food grown in the state, it also helps local farmers. "The challenge with this initiative is finding a product with enough quantity," says Dexter Kishida, Farm to School program specialist. "We need to use anywhere from 10,000 to 15,000 pounds of an ingredient, so we have to see what's available and then figure out a good, creative and feasible way to serve it."[42] This demand for local produce is creating stronger connections between the schools and their suppliers and is helping to sustain the demand for a local and organic farm system for the state of Hawaii, a state which, despite its tropical climate and agricultural history, imports nearly 90 percent of its food.[43]

The hugely innovative Kōkua Kalihi Valley Comprehensive Family Services (KKV), a federally qualified health center in a low-income neighborhood of Honolulu, also uses a farm to connect its community to aina. The farm, a nearly 100-acre parcel at the top of the valley, has a wellness center and a garden that grows many plants indigenous to Hawaii, including pili grass that many youth in the area are using to fashion the roofs of traditionally constructed Hawaiian homes. KKV's medical director, David Derauf, and his staff adopted the philosophy of John Cassel who counseled that the whole neighborhood is the patient.[44] They offer medical and dental care and pharmacy services in addition to providing meeting space for resident-led organizations, a small business that repairs bicycles (providing jobs and free bikes to neighborhood kids), Hawaiian language and culture classes, after-school programs, and many other social services that target the upstream determinants of health.[45]

In a similar John Cassel/whole-community way, the Waianae Coast Comprehensive Health Center (WCCHC) has a campus on the leeward side of Oahu populated by the largest community of Hawaiians in the state. "Long ago, we recognized that addressing the needs of the community needed to go well beyond just providing medical care," according to the vision statement on the clinic's website. WCCHC "addresses health disparities, improves population health, and reduces health inequalities despite financial and cultural barriers."[46] In addition to providing high-quality medical and dental care, WCCHC uses culture and art as a way to improve population health in their community. They host many celebrations and have an artist in residence who uses his sculptures to celebrate the community and inspire it.

Celebrating other aspects of Hawaiian culture is also a way to instill pride and promote a sense of control of one's destiny. Polynesians were the first open ocean seafarers, and relearning that ancient skill was the focus of an effort in 1976 to build a traditional Polynesian ship and sail it from Hawaii to Tahiti. That ship, named the Hōkūle'a, "began as a dream of reviving the legacy of exploration, courage, and ingenuity that brought the first Polynesians to the archipelago of Hawai'i," according to the Polynesian Voyaging Society.[47] "The canoes that brought the first Hawaiians to their island home had disappeared from earth. Cultural extinction felt dangerously close to many Hawaiians when artist Herb Kane dreamed of rebuilding a double-hulled sailing canoe similar to the ones that his ancestors sailed. Though more than six hundred years had passed since the last of these canoes had been seen, this dream brought together people of diverse backgrounds and professions."[48] Today, these voyages traverse the globe and teach the next generation how to sail using these Polynesian seafaring and navigation techniques.

Middle school is such a critical time as children develop, and it has the potential to set the trajectory for the rest of a child's life. That is why it is so disturbing that an estimated 6,000 Hawaiian students in sixth, seventh, and eighth grades (1 of 6) will not graduate from high school without some intervention, according to the Hawaii Community Foundation. That foundation, along with fourteen other funders, supports the Connecting for Success program to provide extra support to students who are having difficulty in school as a strategy to get them to reengage and stay on a path to graduate from high school. This airbag intervention uses "real-time data from the Hawaii State Department of Education's (DOE) Early Warning System to identify struggling students based on their attendance, behavior and course grades."[49] Connecting for Success is part of a larger initiative, Pathways to Resilient Communities.[50]

Connectors

Even if the "buyers" of health were ready and willing to pay for better population health, the actors that can improve health and the "producers of health" are not properly organized to "sell" health to the buyers. We have coordination failure. In order for this marketplace to come into existence, we need "connectors" to help bring the buyers together with the producers. Connectors can use capital and other tools, such as data, to facilitate the connections from buyers to producers. They are the essential ingredient to help this market scale.

Guardrail and airbag investments are large-scale and require the creative participation of the banking and community development finance sectors to bring them to life. They also often require subsidy from all levels of government (federal, state, and local). Banks and CDFIs are particularly adept in financing these transactions. They are great connectors. And the banks in Hawaii, as I mentioned earlier, are not headquartered in far-off capitals; they are homegrown and connected to the communities they serve.

Like in other parts of the country, CRA-motivated banks often work with CDFIs, like the Council for Native Hawaiian Advancement. This twenty-year-old organization provides financing and financial services for Hawaiians.[51] One of the many examples of when they have served as a connector is through a fund to support the 1920 Hawaiian Homes Commission Act that allows Hawaiians to lease government land for $1 per year for a 99-year lease. The problem is that mortgage lenders struggled with how to finance construction and ownership under these unusual conditions. The land is leased, which takes away the central tenet of mortgage lending, the ability to foreclose and reclaim the asset. Without that, the mortgage market withered. And without the ability to finance the homes, the program bogged down. "People die on the waiting list," according to the Kresge Foundation's head of social investing, Joe Evans.[52] The proposed Kukulu Kauhale Fund, which translates as "build a village," is envisioned to ease this process and fix this market failure.

There are thirteen CDFIs in Hawaii playing similar connector roles. Since 1996, they have received over $18 million in funding from the U.S. Treasury's CDFI Fund. And they have received $68 million in New Markets Tax Credit since 2002.[53] As another example of how a CDFI can play the connector role, consider the Local Initiatives Support Corporation (LISC), under the leadership of former CEO Maurice Jones, that sought to create the Hawaii Opportunity Fund—a capital stack. This investment vehicle would be created and operated by LISC, and it would have provided an easier way for buyers of health (health insurers, hospitals, banks, large employers, impact investors, etc.) to pay into the fund that would be used for investing in upstream determinants of health (affordable housing, small businesses, improved food systems, and the like). Tools like this fund ease the process for buyers to invest in health-promoting guardrails and airbags.

And although foundations are often buyers of health, given their ability to take greater financial risk than nearly any other entity, they also serve as important connectors of the market that values health. Foundations—both national and local—can supply the flexible dollars that fill gaps and help bridge multiple streams of public and private financing that do not always line up neatly because they are mismatched in terms of size and have different terms and underwriting requirements.

There are many examples of foundations playing this role but consider one to reduce homelessness in Hawaii—the Housing ASAP program. This program is a connector with an outcomes orientation to "build a statewide network of homeless service providers who will move more homeless families into stable housing faster and help them stay there." This type of intervention requires a network of organizations to provide housing, case management, counseling, job training, and medical care. The producers of health organizations include Catholic Charities Hawaii, Family Life Center, Family Promise of Hawaii, HOPE Services Hawaii, the Institute for Human Services, Kahumana Community/ASI, United States Veterans Initiative, and Waikiki Health. Housing ASAP connects these producers of health with the following buyers: Aloha United Way, American Savings Bank, Bank of Hawaii Foundation, Central Pacific Bank Foundation, Community Housing Fund, Kresge Foundation, Omidyar 'Ohana

Fund, and many other family foundations.[54] Connectors like these point the way to what could be possible when all the available buyer-of-health funds are brought to bear to work on the upstream determinants of health, such as housing, jobs, and physical and mental health.

While we often focus on the financial connectors, another critical connector is the entity that can bring the data together to coordinate, measure, learn, and improve the interventions in the market that values health. Hawaii has many advantages in this area. To start, most of the organizations highlighted in this chapter (e.g., Ma'O Organic Farms, the Early Childhood Action Strategy, and Housing ASAP) are sophisticated users of both data and predictive analytics. And commitment from organizations, universities, government, and philanthropy has created an organization that could play a key role in the market that values health—the Hawaiian Data Collaborative. The Collaborative is motivated by a simple idea and question: "Imagine if you could represent all households and people in Hawaii using a single, simplified dataset. What might such a dataset make possible?"[55] This tool uses U.S. Census data with additional data sources to create a hybrid data tool that can make assessments at multiple levels: individual, family, community, and state. A sophisticated data backbone organization like this one makes it possible to create baselines and measure improvement on multiple levels.

One can imagine taking the use of data a step further, too, as the Waianae Coast Comprehensive Health Center has done with its partner, Foresight Health Solutions. The Health Center had been collecting social determinants of health data on its patients for years but recognized that it was not always actionable. Having the data is one thing, being able to use it to enhance care and reduce costs is another. Foresight Health Solutions was able to bring many new tools to bear, including artificial intelligence and machine learning, to analyze the data and formulate action steps for caregivers. The result was a "unique AI-based risk analytics solution for vulnerable populations that addresses the complex interplay of clinical morbidity (as measured by diagnoses), demographic factors such as age and gender, and most importantly, [social determinants of health] in the determination of future costs and complexity of care," according to Foresight Health Solutions President Ashish Abraham.[56] This new approach used natural language processing tools to analyze millions of sentences in notes in medical records and combine that analysis with other tools such as geospatial analysis. Leinaʻala Kanana, the director of Community Health Services at Waianae Coast Comprehensive Health Center, explained that the Foresight analysis of medical records, insurance claims data, hospital-use data, and other social needs data allows them to triage their patients with risk scores. "We assign the patients having the highest risk to our dedicated care coordination team, along with targeted interventions," according to Kanana. "We use their AI driven solution to predict costs, risks and to improve the health outcomes of our patient population."[57]

Conclusion

This has been a discussion of how one place, Hawaii, could be the place where we break the cake of custom. As you can see, there are many great examples of buyers, producers, and connectors in the state. What could happen next is a market-that-values-health summit where the buyers, producers, and connectors map out a strategy of how dollars could flow from the buyer category to make upstream investments, such as jobs, housing, transportation, education, childhood enrichment, and more. With government and foundations present, these more flexible funding entities could see where the gaps were and find ways to fill them. And over time, a denser network of producers of health would expand their operations to create more guardrails and airbags. As the system grew, we could use data and analysis to see if the interventions were working. Slowly, the "little plans" would accrue to become a big intervention—a market that values health.

This will not be easy work. There are so many competing interests, competing ideas, competing philosophies about what should happen to improve the circumstances of all members of the communities that make up any state or region. It may be that even a relatively small state like Hawaii is too complex to make a true transition to the market that values health. Let the debates and disagreements continue, but in the meantime, is it possible to agree on a few ideas and just keep them working in the background?

> Wouldn't it be better to spend our resources on improving upstream circumstances that support health rather than on expensive and avoidable chronic disease?
>
> Can we target a few simple outcomes that are shared goals for everyone, for example, that all children should arrive at kindergarten ready to learn or that anyone who wants a job should have one?
>
> Can we build this new system in a way that respects local control but also holds local actors accountable for outcomes?

I think the answer to all these questions is yes. But we can also safeguard dissenting views by allowing this to be an opt-in system so that no community feels compelled to participate. As suggested by this chapter, it might make sense to try this new approach in a place like Hawaii and other places with similar attributes. Ideally, over the next ten years, we would have six to ten population-health business model islands in a fee-for-service sea. We would learn if this level of coordination and complexity is possible.

And the advantage of focusing on kids, especially babies, is that we will have results in relatively short order. Six years from now, we will know if the babies born today are all ready to learn at kindergarten. That would be an enormous achievement and might help prove the concept. These island examples (literal and otherwise) of a market that values health are the start. The next task is to create a nationwide version of that market, and that is the subject of chapter 5.

CHAPTER 5

Conclusion and
Next Steps

IN THE COURSE OF THIS BOOK, I have leaned heavily on concepts and examples from economic history to help make the case for how systems come into existence and how they morph into new ones. I think Hawaii, and other places in the United States with similar characteristics, are places where we can solve the wrong pocket problem. They are places where systems can be reoriented to serve new incentives and create better outcomes, similar to how new systems of capital and labor were created in some cities in Northern Europe in the fifteenth and sixteenth centuries. Places like Hawaii suggest that many of the elements are in place to redirect the huge sums we are already spending on downstream consequences of poverty to the upstream determinants of health. These places will be islands of population health business models in a fee-for-service sea. And by doing that, we will not only enjoy a healthier community, but we will also have a fairer and more prosperous society as well.

This new cash flow from the buyers of health will support and expand existing social services and other producers of health. It will also put demand pressure on outcomes and encourage the development of new, and potentially more innovative, producers of health. The demand pressure will also grow the number and types of connectors. This virtuous cycle will build out the actors in this marketplace to the point where all children born in the "islands in a feudal sea" will essentially have a middle-class upbringing guided by guardrails and protected by airbags. This will be good for them, but it will be especially good for their children and grandchildren as we ratchet up aggregate human potential in communities where everyone is supported and no child falls through the cracks.

But how does this spread? Not everyplace is an island. Not everyplace has one, or a few, entities that own the downstream medical care cost risk, which encourages them to invest upstream. How will these communities (most of the country) participate in this new approach to social welfare? I think the jump will look similar to the transition from the first Industrial Revolution (essentially textiles) to the second Industrial Revolution (steel, mass production, mass consumption). Many of the elements will be the same from the first (buyers, producers, and connectors), but new supporting structures in finance, insurance, and technology will take those elements and scale and spread them into a much larger nationwide system.

Making the Jump

After the invention of agriculture, the Industrial Revolution was the most consequential development in human history. But it was many years before those who were experiencing it even realized it was happening; the term *Industrial Revolution* was not widely used until 150 years after the invention of the steam engine.[1] That is an important lesson in itself: revolutions are hard to see when you are in the middle of them. The first Industrial Revolution took place around 1740–1780 and primarily focused on textiles. It was relatively small in scale, and almost every aspect of it required building new ways of doing things, or new systems. For example, the first factory in the United States was built by Samuel Slater in Pawtucket, Rhode Island. It used the power generated from a waterwheel to produce cloth and clothing. But it was unclear how the labor would be organized (e.g., whole families were hired as a unit of labor), there was no way to raise capital by selling stock, and there were few legal examples for how to organize the firm or protect workers. All these processes had to be invented, along with new ways to ship raw materials and finished products, market and sell those products, insure the process from calamity, and more.

The second Industrial Revolution took place over 100 years later, in the late nineteenth century, and reorganized economic life on a massive scale. It was dominated by steel, shipbuilding, locomotives, chemicals, pharmaceuticals, consumer goods, and, later, automobiles. The scale dwarfed the first Industrial Revolution, but the structure followed the early model closely. In other words, the financial, legal, and organizational systems that were developed for textiles provided the framework for the massive expansion of a new way of managing resources and the economy. The result was the most substantial gain in the standard of living the world had ever seen.

We need an antipoverty industry that matches the scale and reach of the second Industrial Revolution. I think community development finance provided that first Industrial Revolution framework. And the market that values health will build on that framework and reach the scale and scope of the second Industrial Revolution. More than a trillion dollars every year flowing to guardrails and airbags for every community in America will create hope for millions, dramatically improve the health of the nation, and create more prosperity for all.

As a starting point, the nationwide market that values health must find a way to simulate the condition where one entity owns the downstream medical care cost risk for a community. Most places do not have just one (or a few) buyers of health, but all the many owners of that risk could be pooled. The many buyers of health could join together and pay into an upstream-buyers-of-health pooled fund in the same proportions that they own the downstream risk. So, in a hypothetical example, you could have a metro area where ten entities each owned 10 percent of the downstream medical care cost risk. None of those entities have the incentive to make upstream investments because the likelihood of recouping those investments is small. This environment is not like Maui, where people often stay in one place for a lifetime—there is a lot of churn. The composition of one entity's 10 percent is in constant flux, and as existing members leave and new ones come into that entity's system, those new arrivals did not benefit from guardrail and airbag investments. Here the market fails.

The pooled fund would be used to pay producers of health to focus their efforts on 100 percent of the metro population—so that all the metro area would be covered. All the citizens in this community would enjoy guardrail and airbag investments. All the producers of health in this area would have adequate funding to ensure that the social safety net was strong.

The twin pillars of a market that values health—the sources for its demand—are population health business models and Pay for Success financing for social programs. Reorienting the existing social service sector around outcomes is an additional source of funding for guard-rails and airbags. Even if a relatively small percentage of existing an-tipoverty funding is redirected to this approach, it will be an early investor in the buyer of health category. This will put added demand pressure for the producers of health to up their game. These two strategies—population health business models and Pay for Success financing—are just two ways the island-breakthrough-communities could spread to become a nationwide system.

As this approach to social services grew and began to demonstrate results, significant new resources would flow to it. This will create new opportunities to transform the finance system to provide more liquid-ity and flexibility for the investments in upstream health. Today, those investments are disjointed, small, and heterogeneous. There has never been an opportunity for the geniuses on Wall Street to figure out a way to bring their services to this sector. But if you can imagine that there are now hundreds of billions of dollars invested in Ready-to-Learn-by-Kindergarten Bonds, for example, there might be a way to create a secondary market for those investments.

A secondary market for social investments has been something of a Holy Grail for social investors for fifty years. The secondary market for mortgages, for example, brings down cost, provides liquidity, spreads risks effectively (in most cases before and after the mortgage-fueled market crash in 2008), and brings the dream of owning a home to millions more people. What if there were a secondary market for the financial assets of the market that values health? What if there were a Fannie Mae for health?[2]

The impediment to date for the secondary market for social investments has been these three obstacles: (1) too few transactions (scale), (2) too little data to model risk and return, and (3) lack of standardization in transactions (legal documents, terms, etc.). When we reach the scale of the national market that values health, all three problems are solved for investments in improving health. These investments in schools, clinics, libraries, and airbag interventions that improve life chances will dwarf the existing social finance market. Greater scale will bring more data and incentivize standardization of transactions. We will all be better off when Wall Street brings its talents to finance improved health and wellbeing.

I recognize that the belief in the benefits that flow from increased demand is not magic. But the power of effective economic demand is hard to dismiss. The ancient Greeks conceptually understood how steam engines worked two thousand years before the first engines were built. But why build one if there isn't an economic reason to do so? It is no accident that James Watt developed the modern steam engine following what Berkeley professor Jan DeVries calls the "Industrious Revolution" in the early 1600s. The Industrious Revolution describes how people in Northern Europe and preindustrial Japan were increasingly willing to work harder and smarter to improve their material conditions. As people worked longer hours, they began to free up an economic surplus. That surplus was the early demand for the breakthroughs in production technology, like the steam engine, interchangeable parts, assembly lines, and all the other breakthroughs of the early

Industrial Revolution in the early 1700s.[3] Technological innovation was in response to economic demand.

The market that values health will similarly put demand pressure on innovating around technology. In the course of this book, we have seen new technology platforms that help organize, coordinate, and analyze interventions to help veterans (Unite US), help homeless people get off the street in Santa Clara County (Palantir's Project Welcome Home), and create sophisticated complex adaptive systems software that helps identify key interventions (Kumu). As we think through the possibilities here, there may be ways to use the open-ledger technology of blockchain to take these platforms to even higher levels, where we have more sophisticated case management for anyone needing services with no risk to privacy.

In addition to these platforms, the need for timely, granular, and actionable data will be paramount. Here we see the outlines of what is to come modeled on innovative programs, such as the Hawaii Data Collaborative, or innovative use of artificial intelligence as in the example of Lyric's response to clients' mental health service needs. In the end, we are better off when Silicon Valley also brings its talents to improve health and wellbeing.

Conclusion

In this book, I have been critical of many prior, and existing, social welfare policies and programs. Some people interpret that as an attack and an argument to not try. Nothing could be further from the truth. I am critical because I have taken to heart the advice of the Orthodox monk in *The Brothers Karamazov*, who counsels, "Above all, don't lie to yourself. The man who lies to himself and listens to his own lie comes to a point that he cannot distinguish the truth within him, or around him, and so loses all respect for himself and for others." We need to be clear-eyed in our assessments of prior efforts. If they don't work, we must learn from that. Take what elements seemed to work, and try something new—innovate, fail, and iterate again. Only by fearlessly engaging in this dialectic will we arrive at new syntheses that are more effective.

To that end, we know most place-based policies have failed to achieve their goals of inclusive opportunity-rich communities for all. And most people-based policies, especially those aimed at the down-stream social needs like drug and alcohol addiction, homelessness, or job training, are rarely successful. That does not mean we should just stop trying because nothing works. We know that some combination of place-based and people-based policies must be the answer to help all people reach their potential, or, in other words, to experience the Fifth Freedom. While there is a lot of research confirming this, most of us know it already because we have experienced it. What is particularly effective about the market that values health is that it allows us to try ever-changing configurations of policies and interventions in multiple places, responding to the needs of each place in real time. It is a process, not a program.

And as we try many more strategies, and track them using data and rigorous analysis, our understanding of what tools work, at what times, and with which populations, will also grow. We are just scratching the surface of that world of knowledge. And this reality is nothing to be ashamed of; we are simply new at trying to take care of each other on a massive scale. As I outlined in chapter 1, this work has only started in earnest since the 1880s. We have a lot to learn, and a little humility in that process will serve us well.

Pablo Neruda, in his Nobel lecture, said, "Lastly, I wish to say to the people of good will, to the workers, to the poets, that the whole future has been expressed in this line by Rimbaud: 'only with a burning patience can we conquer the splendid City which will give light, justice and dignity to all mankind.'"[4] We must burn with the desire to do better, while being patient since we do not always know how to build those splendid cities. Slowly and inexorably, we will get there. We will not always agree with each other on how to do it. Disagreements are good. That is how we develop a deeper understanding and weed out ideas that don't work. In the end, however, those gleaming communities will be places of "light, justice and dignity," where all children enjoy the fifth freedom—a right to an open future and the opportunity to reach their full potential.

Notes

Preface

1. *Community Development Investment Review* 5, no. 3 (2009), https://www.frbsf
   .org/community-development/files/cdreview_issue3_09.pdf.
2. Risa Lavizzo-Mourey, "Why Health, Poverty, and Community Development
   Are Inseparable," *Investing in What Works for America's Communities* (San Francisco:
   Federal Reserve Bank of San Francisco and the Low Income Investment Fund,
   2012), 224.

Introduction

1. Jodi Halpern and others, "Social Dominance, School Bullying, and Child Health:
   What Are Our Ethical Obligations to the Very Young?" *Pediatrics* 135, supple-
   ment 2 (2015): S24–30. doi:10.154/peds.2014-3549C.
2. Halpern and others, S28.
3. Robert D. Putnam, *OUR KIDS: The American Dream in Crisis* (New York: Simon
   & Schuster, 2015).
4. This book was also inspired by a book chapter I wrote in 2017. Many ideas and
   some text from the book chapter are reprinted throughout this book. David Erickson, "The March Toward Outcomes-Focused Financing," in *What Matters: Investing in Results to Build Strong, Vibrant Communities* (San Francisco: The Federal
   Reserve Bank of San Francisco and the Nonprofit Finance Fund, 2017), 29–54.
5. *Investing in What Works for America's Communities* (San Francisco: The Federal
   Reserve Bank of San Francisco and Low Income Investment Fund, 2012); *What
   Counts* (San Francisco: The Federal Reserve Bank of San Francisco and the Urban
   Institute, 2014); *What It's Worth* (San Francisco: The Federal Reserve Bank of San
   Francisco and Prosperity Now, 2015); *Investing in What Matters* (San Francisco:
   The Federal Reserve Bank of San Francisco and Nonprofit Finance Fund, 2017).
6. Tyler Norris, Well Being Trust, cites this idea often. For more details on this idea,
   see Amy Shields, "Thriving Together: A Springboard for Equitable Recovery and
   Resilience in Communities Across America," Well Being Trust, July 27, 2020.
7. World Health Organization, Constitution of the World Health Organization as
   adopted by the International Health Conference, New York, June 19–22, 1946;

signed on July 22, 1946, by the representatives of 61 states (Official Records of the World Health Organization, no. 2, 100) and entered into force on April 7, 1948. In Frank P. Grad, "The Preamble of the Constitution of the World Health Organization," *Bulletin of the World Health Organization: The International Journal of Public Health* 80, no. 12 (2002): 982.

8. Andre Perry, Jonathan Rothwell, and David Harshbarger, *The Devaluation of Assets in Black Neighborhoods: The Case of Residential Properties* (Brookings Institution, 2018).

9. Data are available at Opportunity Insights, National Trends, "The American Dream Is Fading."

10. Alexandre Tanzi, "America's Upper Middle Class Feeling the Pinch Too," Bloomberg News, April 13, 2019.

11. Anthony Salvanto and others, "Americans Optimistic about Economy, But Pessimistic about Country's Direction—CBS News Poll."

12. UC Davis Center for Poverty Research, "What Is 'Deep Poverty?'" (UC Davis Center for Poverty Research, 2018).

13. Ajay Chaudry and others, "Poverty in the United States: 50-Year Trends and Safety Net Impacts" (U.S. Department of Health and Human Services, March 2016).

14. Emily A. Shrider and others, "Income and Poverty in the United States: 2020" September 14, 2021, Report Number P60-273 (U.S. Census Bureau, 2021), Table B-1. People in Poverty by Selected Characteristics: 2019 and 2020.

15. Shrider and others, "Income and Poverty." For an interesting discussion of civic renewal, see Robert D. Putnam and Shaylyn Romney Garrett, *The Upswing: How America Came Together a Century Ago and How We Can Do It Again* (New York: Simon & Schuster, 2020).

16. Robert Greenstein, "Commentary: Universal Basic Income May Sound Attractive but, If It Occurred, Would Likelier Increase Poverty Than Reduce It," Center on Budget and Policy Priorities, June 13, 2019.

17. It is true that a small percentage of the population accounts for an outsized proportion of medical care spending; the top 5 percent of spenders consume nearly half of all medical care dollars. But we know that these "high utilizers" alone cannot explain the trend entirely, especially because most health outcomes have little to do with medical care. Something else is going on.

18. For life expectancy declines, see Centers for Disease Control and Prevention, "National Vital Statistics Reports" (Centers for Disease Control and Prevention, various years); and S. H. Woolf and H. Schoomaker, "Life Expectancy and Mortality Rates in the United States, 1959–2017," *Journal of the American Medical Association* 322, no. 20 (2019). White non-Hispanics in midlife (ages forty-five to fifty-four) have been hit particularly hard, especially those without a high school education, which Anne Case and Angus Deaton attribute to deaths

of despair from suicide, drug abuse, and liver disease from loss of jobs, declining wages, and other economic and societal changes. Anne Case and Angus Deaton, "Rising Morbidity and Mortality in Midlife among White Non-Hispanic Americans in the 21st Century," *Proceedings of the National Academy of Sciences* 112, no. 49 (December 8, 2015): 15078–83. See also Anne Case and Angus Deaton, "Mortality and Morbidity in the 21st Century," Brookings Papers on Economic Activity (Spring 2017).

19. The U.S. homicide rate in 2018 was 5/100,000 people, down from 10.2 in 1980. The homicide rate declined sharply from 9.3/100,000 in 1992 to 4.8 in 2010. See Federal Bureau of Investigation, "Crime in the United States, 2018," Criminal Justice Information Services Division, 2018. See also, FBI National Press Office, "FBI Releases 2018 Crime Statistics," press release, September 20, 2019; and Alexia Cooper and Erica L. Smith, "Homicide Trends in the United States, 1980–2008, Annual Rates for 2009 and 2010" (U.S. Department of Justice, 2008).

20. By 2000, age-adjusted mortality rates from heart disease had declined to about one-third of their 1960s baseline. George A. Mensah and others, "Decline in Cardiovascular Mortality: Possible Causes and Implications," *Circulation Research* 120, no. 2 (2017).

21. HIV/AIDS deaths declined from a peak of more than 40,000 in 1995 to approximately 10,000 in 2013. Since 2015, the decline has slowed. C. Murray and others, "Global, Regional, and National Incidence and Mortality for HIV, Tuberculosis, and Malaria during 1990–2013: A Systematic Analysis for the Global Burden of Disease Study 2013," *Lancet* 384, no. 9947 (2014): 1005–70.

22. Holly Hedegaard, Sally C. Curtin, and Margaret Warner, "Increase in Suicide Mortality in the United States, 1999–2018," NCHS Data Brief, No. 362, April 2020.

23. Steven H. Woolf, Ryan K. Masters, and Laudan Y. Aron, "Effect of the COVID-19 Pandemic in 2020 on Life Expectancy across Populations in the USA and Other High Income Countries: Simulations of Provisional Mortality Data," *BMJ* 373, no. 1343 (June 24, 2021), doi.org/10.1136/bmj.n1343.

24. Max Roser, "The Link between Health Spending and Life Expectancy: The US Is an Outlier," Our World in Data, May 26, 2017. Also see an earlier version, Max Roser, "The Link between Health Spending and Life Expectancy: The US Is an Outlier," Institute for New Economic Thinking, August 18, 2016.

25. David H. Freedman, "Health Care's 'Upstream' Conundrum," *Politico*, January 10, 2018.

26. Christopher Howard, *The Hidden Welfare State: Tax Expenditures and Social Policy in the United States* (Princeton University Press, 1997), 17.

27. Howard, *The Hidden Welfare State*, 27 and 25.

28. Organization for Economic Cooperation and Development (OECD), "Social Expenditure Update, 2019" (Paris, France: OECD, January 2019).

29. Social Expenditure Database (SOCX), www.oecd.org/social/expenditure.htm.

30. Kimberly J. Morgan, "How the Country Could Get More for Less," *Foreign Affairs*, January/February 2013, 153–54.

31. Social Expenditure Database (SOCX), U.S. GDP, Bureau of Economic Analysis, table 1.1.5, 2015 Gross Domestic Product, 2019. Data sources for negative downstream expenditures: Criminal justice expenditures and victimization: U.S. Bureau of Justice Statistics, table 1, all government expenditures for total justice system, 2015, and the National Crime Victimization Survey, 2015, 2016, and 2017 Public-Use Files. U.S. Federal Bureau of Investigation, Unified Crime Reporting, tables 1 and 12, 2018; Kathryn E. McCollister, Michael T. French, and Hai Fang, "The Cost of Crime to Society: New Crime-Specific Estimates for Policy and Program Evaluation," *Drug and Alcohol Dependence* 108, no. 1–2 (January 13, 2010): 98–109, doi:10.1016/j.drugalcdep.2009.12.002; Table 3, 2010 Special education: Digest of Education Statistics, 2017 (NCES 2018-070), National Center for Education Statistics, tables 236.10, 236.55, 2018. The U.S. Department of Education, National Center for Education Statistics, 2019, Chapter 2; Special Education Expenditure Project (SEEP), "What Are We Spending on Special Education Services in the United States, 1999–2000?" June 2004; Lost worker productivity: US Chamber of Commerce, "The Economic Cost of Disease," June 25, 2018.

    Notes: Data on the number of occurrences of crimes are from 2017; all other data are from 2015 or the 2015–2016 school year. To estimate total special education expenditures, ECONorthwest multiplied 2015–2016 current expenditures per student by the ratio of special education expenditures per special education student to current expenditures per regular student as reported in SEEP, "What Are We Spending?," then multiplied the result by the total number of students enrolled in special education in 2015–2016. Special education estimates do not account for private spending.

    ECONorthwest estimated the 2015 cost of victimization using McCollister, French, and Fang, "The Cost of Crime to Society," 2010, which estimated the cost of crime to society. In that analysis, the authors include tangible victim costs for murder, rape or sexual assault, aggravated assault, robbery, motor vehicle theft, arson, household burglary, and larceny or theft. McCollister and colleagues' per crime estimates were converted into 2015 dollars and multiplied by the number of occurrences of each crime in the United States to arrive at an estimate of the total cost of victimization as a share of GDP.

32. Katherine Linzer, Jaana Remes, and Shubham Singhal, "How Prioritizing Health Is a Prescription for US Prosperity," McKinsey Global Institute, October 5, 2020.

33. Linzer, Remes, and Singhal. Sadly, the McKinsey report focuses its search for solutions from medical interventions, rather than what we know will make the country healthier—more guardrails and airbags. Also see Simiao Chen and

others, "The Macroeconomic Burden of Noncommunicable Diseases in the United States: Estimates and Projections," November 1, 2018, doi:10.1371/journal.pone.0206702.

34. Raj Chetty and others, "Where Is the Land of Opportunity? The Geography of Intergenerational Mobility in the United States," NBER Working Paper No. 19843, January 2014, rev. June 2014, 10.3386/w19843. *PloS ONE* 13, no. 11 (November 1, 2018), https://www.nber.org/papers/w19843. Also see Isabel V. Sawhill and John E. Morton, *Economic Mobility: Is the American Dream Alive and Well?* Brookings Institution, Report of the Economic Mobility Project, 2007.

35. Chetty and others, "Where Is the Land of Opportunity?"

36. David Callahan, "Systemic Failure: Four Reasons Philanthropy Keeps Losing the Battle against Inequality," *Inside Philanthropy*, January 10, 2018.

37. Ninety percent of the nation's $3.5 trillion in annual health care expenditures is for chronic disease and mental health conditions. Christine Buttorff, Teague Ruder, and Melissa Bauman, *Multiple Chronic Conditions in the United States*, RAND, 2017; Centers for Medicare & Medicaid Services, "National Health Expenditures 2017 Highlights," CMS, n.d. Heart disease and stroke cost approximately $200 billion per year. E. J. Benjamin and others, "Heart Disease and Stroke Statistics—2018 Update: A Report from the American Heart Association," *Circulation* 137 (2018): e67–e492. Diabetes costs the U.S. health care system and employers $237 billion every year. American Diabetes Association, "Economic Costs of Diabetes in the U.S. in 2017," *Diabetes Care* 41, no. 5 (2018): 917–28. Obesity costs the U.S. health care system $147 billion a year. E. A. Finkelstein and others, "Annual Medical Spending Attributable to Obesity: Payer- and Service-Specific Estimates," *Health Affairs* 28, no. 5 (2009): 822–31. The total cost attributable to arthritis and related conditions was about $304 billion in 2013. Centers for Disease Control and Prevention, "The Cost of Arthritis in US Adults," CDC, 2013. The cost of treating Alzheimer's in 2010 was approximately $215 billion. M. D. Hurd and others, "Monetary Costs of Dementia in the United States," *New England Journal of Medicine* 368, no. 14 (2013): 1326–34.

38. Jane Goodman and Claire Conway, "Poor Health: When Poverty Becomes Disease," *Patient Care* (January 6, 2016).

39. Elizabeth H. Bradley and others, "Variation in Health Outcomes: The Role of Spending on Social Services, Public Health, and Health Care, 2000–09," *Health Affairs* 35, no. 5 (May 2016): 760.

40. For a robust discussion of the ways to measure annual antipoverty expenditures in the United States, see H. Luke Shaefer, Kate Naranjo, and David Harris, "Spending on Government Anti-Poverty Efforts: Healthcare Expenditures Vastly Outstrip Income Transfers." University of Michigan, September 2019.

41. For more on this argument, see the distinction between social needs versus social determinants as explored by Brian Castrucci and John Auerbach, "Meeting

Individual Social Needs Falls Short of Addressing Social Determinants of Health," Health Affairs *Forefront* (blog), January 16, 2019.

42. Bryan Stevenson, *Just Mercy: A Story of Justice and Redemption* (New York: Spiegel & Grau, 2014), 89–90.

43. I first heard this title given to the idea of a population-health business model from Kevin Jones, cofounder of the SoCap conference series.

44. David Erickson, "The March toward Outcomes-Based Financing," in *What Matters: Investing in Results to Build Strong, Vibrant Communities* (San Francisco: Federal Reserve Bank of San Francisco and the Nonprofit Finance Fund, 2017), 36.

45. The *Ur* example of this sort of superperson intervention powered with help from rich friends is the story of Geoffrey Canada and Harlem Childrens' Zone. See Paul Tough, *Whatever It Takes: Geoffrey Canada's Quest to Change Harlem and America* (Boston: Houghton Mifflin, 2008).

46. Anne C. Kubisch and others, *Voices from the Field III: Lessons and Challenges from Two Decades of Community Change Efforts* (Washington, DC: Aspen Institute, 2010).

47. Center for Community Health and Evaluation, "Changing Systems in Community Development: Lessons from the First Three Years of the Strong, Prosperous, and Resilient Communities Challenge (SPARCC)," April 2020.

48. Elizabeth A. Duke, "Foreword: Building Sustainable Communities," *Investing in What Works for America's Communities* (San Francisco: Federal Reserve Bank of San Francisco and Low Income Investment Fund, 2012), 1.

49. This typology was created by Ian Galloway, vice president and regional executive, Federal Reserve Bank of San Francisco, for a conference in 2014 called "SOCAP Health" at the New York Academy of Medicine. More information on that conference is available at Lindsay Smalling, "SOCAP Health: Creating the Market That Values Health," May 30, 2014, socapglobal.com/2014/05/so-cap -health/.

50. Jesse M. Pines and others, "Maryland's Experiment with Capitated Payments for Rural Hospitals: Large Reductions in Hospital-Based Care," *Health Affairs* 38, no. 4 (April 2019).

51. Frances Campbell and others, "Early Childhood Investments Substantially Boost Adult Health," *Science* 343 (2014). See also The Heckman Equation, "Research Summary: Abecedarian & Health," n.d.

52. E. E. Werner and R. S. Smith, *Overcoming the Odds: High-Risk Children from Birth to Adulthood* (Cornell University Press, 1992).

53. For a detailed discussion of these, and many other Pay for Success tools, see *What Matters: Investing in Results to Build Strong, Vibrant Communities* (San Francisco: Federal Reserve Bank of San Francisco and Nonprofit Finance Fund, 2017).

54. Maggie Super Church, "Building the Market for Healthy Neighborhoods," Build Healthy Places Network, November 11, 2014.

55. United Way of Hawaii, "ALICE in Hawai'i: A Financial Hardship Study," 2020, ii.

56. Kristen Consillio, "Hawaii Hospitals Move Services to Outpatient Facilities," *Star Advertiser*, May 20, 2019.

Chapter 1. Evolution of the Welfare State

1. Library of Congress, *Civil War Desk Reference* (New York: Simon & Schuster, 2002), 74.
2. U.S. Census, "The Urban Population as a Percentage of the Total Population by U.S. Region and State (1790–1990)."
3. U.S. Census, "The Urban Population."
4. United Nations Population Fund, *State of World Population 2007: Unleashing the Potential of Urban Growth* (New York: United Nations Population Fund, 2007), 1.
5. Mary Ann Johnson, "Hull House," in *The Encyclopedia of Chicago*, ed. James R. Grossman, Ann Durkin Keating, and Janice L. Reiff (University of Chicago Press, 2004), 402.
6. David M. Kennedy, *The American People in the Great Depression: Freedom from Fear, Part One* (Oxford University Press, 1999), 163.
7. Franklin D. Roosevelt, Inaugural Address, January 20, 1937. Available at: https://avalon.law.yale.edu/20th_century/froos2.asp.
8. Kennedy, 88.
9. "The White Angel Bread Line" by Dorothea Lange, San Francisco, California, 1933; Records of the Social Security Administration; Record Group 47; National Archives, https://www.archives.gov/historical-docs/todays-doc/?dod-date=1029.
10. Robert D. Plotnick and others, "The Twentieth-Century Record of Inequality and Poverty in the United States," Discussion Paper No. 1166-98 (Madison, WI: Institute for Research on Poverty, July 1998), 21.
11. Andrew Glyn and others, *The Rise and Fall of the Golden Age of Capitalism: Reinterpreting the Postwar Experience* (Oxford University Press, 1990).
12. More information is available on the Supplemental Poverty Measure at https://www.census.gov/library/publications/2021/demo/p60-275.html#:~:text=Beginning%20in%202011%2C%20the%20U.S.,in%20the%20official%20poverty%20measure.
13. Lyndon Johnson, Remarks at the Johnson County Courthouse, Paintsville, Kentucky, 1964. The American Presidency Project at the University of California, Santa Barbara, http://www.presidency.ucsb.edu/ws/?pid=26190.
14. James T. Patterson, *Grand Expectations: The United States, 1945–1974* (Oxford University Press, 1996), 538.
15. Alan Brinkley, *The Unfinished Nation: A Concise History of the American People*, 4th ed. (New York: McGraw Hill, 2004).
16. Patterson, *Grand Expectations*, 539–40.
17. John Cassel, "The Contribution of the Social Environment to Host Resistance," *American Journal of Epidemiology* 104, no. 2 (1976): 107–23.

18. Address to a convention of the National League of Cities by HUD secretary Robert Weaver, March 30, 1966. Record Group 207, Federal Archives, College Park, Maryland.

19. Social Security Amendments of 1965, https://www.govinfo.gov/content/pkg /STATUTE-79/pdf/STATUTE-79-Pg286.pdf#page=1.

20. Karen Mossberger, *From Gray Areas to New Communities: Lessons and Issues from Comprehensive Neighborhood Initiative* (Great Cities Institute, University of Illinois at Chicago, 2010).

21. Scott Kohler, "Bedford-Stuyvesant and the Rise of the Community Development Corporation," Case Study 33 (Duke University Sanford School of Public Policy, Center for Strategic Philanthropy and Society, 1966).

22. Avis Vidal, *Rebuilding Communities: A National Study of Urban Community Development Corporations* (New York: New School for Social Research, 1992), 2.

23. National Congress for Community Economic Development (NCCED), "Reaching New Heights" (NCCED, June 2006), 4.

24. Clifford Rosenthal, *Democratizing Finance: Origins of the Community Development Finance Institutions Movement* (Victoria, BC: Friesen Press, 2018).

25. CDFI Fund, U.S. Treasury. Exact numbers available at https://www.cdfifund.gov /programs-training/certification/cdfi/Pages/default.aspx.

26. Luis G. Dopico, "20 Years of CDFI Banks and Credit Unions: 1996–2015: An Analysis of Trends and Growth" (Philadelphia, PA: Opportunity Finance Network, January 31, 2017).

27. Opportunity Finance Network, "What Is a CDFI?," https://ofn.org/what-cdfi. See also, Adam DeRose, "CDFIs: The Financial Institutions You're Not Covering," National Center for Business Journalism, November 19, 2015.

28. The process of coalescing and then disbanding to join again in a new configuration with new partners provides the opportunity to learn from mistakes. It guards against turf battles and the sclerosis that can set into traditional bureaucratic institutions. It allows flexibility in the response to a problem, so that if the need arises for more expertise in a particular area, such as education, health, or crime prevention, other groups or institutions with those skills or knowledge can join the network. David J. Erickson, *Housing Policy Revolution: Networks and Neighborhoods* (Urban Institute, 2009), 157.

29. David J. Erickson, "The March toward Outcomes-Based Funding," in *What Matters: Investing in Results to Build Strong, Vibrant Communities* (San Francisco: Federal Reserve Bank of San Francisco and the Nonprofit Finance Fund, 2017), 29–54.

30. For more information on HOLC maps from the New Deal, see the Mapping Inequality project. Robert K. Nelson and others, "Mapping Inequality," in *American Panorama*, ed. Robert K. Nelson and Edward L. Ayers, https://dsl.richmond

.edu/panorama/redlining/#loc=4/35.711/-108.018&text=about. The Los Angeles map is available at https://s3.amazonaws.com/holc/tiles/CA/LosAngeles1 /1939/holc-scan.jpg. There is some interesting recent analysis by researchers at the Federal Reserve Bank of Chicago that suggests the Federal Housing Administration (FHA) had more influence restricting loans to Black borrowers than the HOLC maps did (started earlier and lasted longer). See Price Fishback and others, "New Evidence on Redlining by Federal Housing Programs in the 1930s" (Working Paper, January 3, 2022, WP 2022-01), doi:10.21033/wp-2022-01.

31. Federal Reserve Board of Governors, "What Is the CRA?"

32. Laurie Goodman, Jun Zhu, and John Walsh, "The Community Reinvestment Act: What Do We Know, and What Do We Need to Know?" (Working Paper, Urban Institute, August 30, 2019). See also Laurie Goodman, Jun Zhu, and John Walsh, "The Community Reinvestment Act: What Do We Know, and What Do We Need to Know?" *Housing Policy Debate* 30, no. 1 (2020): 83–100, doi:10.108 0/10511482.2019.1665837.

33. Clifford Rosenthal, *Democratizing Finance: Origins of the Community Development Financial Institutions Movement* (Altona, MB: Friesen Press, 2018), 250–51.

34. Maria Martinez-Cosio and Mike R. Bussel, *Catalysts for Change: 21st Century Philanthropy and Community Change* (New York: Routledge, 2013).

35. Jordan Rappaport, "U.S. Urban Decline and Growth, 1950 to 2000," in *Economic Review* (Third Quarter 2003): 15–42.

36. Rappaport, 16–17.

37. Katharine L. Bradbury, Anthony Downs, and Kenneth A. Small, *Urban Decline and the Future of American Cities* (The Brookings Institution, 1982).

38. Michael J. Rich and Robert P. Stoker, *Collaborative Governance for Urban Revitalization: Lessons from Empowerment Zones* (Cornell University Press, 2014), 1.

39. David Wright and others, *Building a Community Plan for Strategic Change: Findings from the First Round Assessment of the Empowerment Zone/Enterprise Community Initiative* (Rockefeller Institute of Government, State University of New York, 1996).

40. Rich and Stoker, *Collaborative Governance*, 7.

41. Susan J. Popkin and others, *A Decade of HOPE VI: Research Findings and Policy Challenges* (Urban Institute, 2004).

42. Popkin and others, 48.

43. Anne Kubisch, *Voices from the Field III: Lessons and Challenges from Two Decades of Community Change Efforts* (Washington, DC: Aspen Institute, 2010), 10.

44. Anne C. Kubisch and others, "Community Change Initiatives from 1990–2010: Accomplishments and Implications for Future Work," Federal Reserve Bank of San Francisco, *Community Investments* (Spring 2010): 8–12, 36.

45. Kubisch and others, 10.

46. Kubisch and others, 12.

47. Paul C. Brophy and Rachel D. Godsil, *Retooling HUD for a Catalytic Federal Government: A Report to Secretary Shaun Donovan* (University of Pennsylvania Institute for Urban Research, February 2009).

48. John Kania and Mark Kramer, "Collective Impact," *Stanford Social Innovation Review* 9, no. 2 (Winter 2011): 36–41.

49. Urban Institute and MDRC, *Choice Neighborhoods: Baseline Conditions and Early Progress*, September 2015; Kania and Kramer, "Collective Impact," iii.

50. Kania and Kramer, "Collective Impact," iv.

51. Kania and Kramer, 7.

52. Kania and Kramer, xvii.

53. Urban Institute and MDRC, *Choice Neighborhoods*, xi.

54. International City/County Management Association, "Evaluating the Role of Local Government and Project Stakeholder Engagement in Choice Neighborhoods Transformation Planning and Implementation," December 1, 2015, https:// icma.org/documents/evaluating-role-local-government-and-project-stakeholder -engagement-choice-neighborhoods-transformation-planning-and-imple mentation.

55. U.S. Government Accountability Office, *Education Grants: Promise Neighborhoods Promotes Collaboration but Needs National Evaluation Plan*, Report to the Chairman, Committee on Education and the Workforce, House of Representatives, May 2014, GAO-14-432, 1.

56. Paul Tough, "The Way We Live Now: 24/7 School Reform," *New York Times Magazine*, September 5, 2008.

57. And even the claims of success of the Harlem Children's Zone are controversial; an early analysis of the HCZ program by Brookings researchers found "no compelling evidence that investments in parenting classes, health services, nutritional programs, and community improvement in general have appreciable effects on student achievement." These findings are still controversial a decade later as the debate rages in the education community between the schools-only intervention versus the broader-neighborhood intervention factions. See Grover J. Whitehurst and Michelle Croft, "The Harlem Children's Zone, Promise Neighborhoods, and the Broader, Bolder Approach to Education," July 20, 2010, Brown Center on Education Policy at Brookings.

58. Urban Institute, "Creating Lasting Change through Community Leadership: How Promise Neighborhoods Are Working with Residents to Weather Crises and Transform Communities," December 1, 2020.

59. Urban Institute, 4.

60. Andrew Ujifusa, "How Have Obama's K–12 Policies Fared under Trump?" *Education Week*, June 19, 2018, https://www.edweek.org/policy-politics/how-have -obamas-k-12-policies-fared-under-trump/2018/06.

61. Amadou Diallo, "As Harlem Children's Zone Moves to Export Its Model Nationwide, Other City Programs Offer Cautionary Tales," *Washington Post*, December 21, 2020.

62. For a summary on the complexity of mapping the many sources of funds necessary to keep the pipeline functioning properly, see Matthew J. Joseph and Lori Connors-Tadros, *Sustaining Community Revitalization: A Tool for Mapping Funds for Promise Neighborhood Initiatives*, The Finance Project, August 2011.

63. *Scaling Up a Place-Based Employment Program: Highlights from the Jobs Plus Pilot Program Evaluation*, Prepared for U.S. Department of Housing and Urban Development, Office of Policy Development and Research, September 2017.

64. For more information, see the Jobs Plus Initiative Program website: https://www .hud.gov/program_offices/public_indian_housing/jpi.

65. *Scaling Up a Place-Based Employment Program*, vi.

66. James Ross and Andrea Martone, "National Collaborative Announces $80 million Investment in Five Cities," Press Release, Living Cities, October 28, 2010.

67. JaNay Queen Nazaire, *The Integration Initiative—Systems Change for Economic Mobility & Equity: Lessons from the Field* (Research Triangle Park, NC: RTI International, December 2019).

68. For more about SPARCC, see https://www.sparcchub.org/about/; California Endowment's overview of its Build Healthy Places work can be found at https:// www.buildinghealthycommunities.org/; for an overview of strategy and partners for HOPE SF, see https://www.hope-sf.org/.

69. Margery Austin Turner and others, "Tackling Persistent Poverty in Distressed Urban Neighborhoods: History, Principles and Strategies for Philanthropic Investments," Urban Institute, July 2014.

70. James M. Ferris and Elwood Hopkins, "Place-Based Initiatives: Lessons from Five Decades of Experimentation and Experience," *Foundation Review* 7, no. 4 (December 2015): 107, doi.org/10.9707/1944-5660.1269.

71. Meir Rinde, "Did the Comprehensive Community Initiatives of the 1990s, Early 2000s Bring About Change? Once a Must-Have for Foundations, Comprehensive Community Initiatives Found Mixed Success," *Shelterforce*, March 15, 2021.

72. Hord/Caplan/Macht, *Johnston Square Vision Plan*, Rebuild Metro, February 14, 2020, 40.

73. Purpose Built Communities, https://purposebuiltcommunities.org/how-we-work/.

74. Bayou District Foundation Impact Report 2020, LifeCity, 2020, https://bayoudis trictfoundation.com/impact-report-2020/; East Lake Foundation 2021 Annual Report, East Lake Foundation, 2022, https://www.eastlakefoundation.org/annual -reports/2021/; and the 2019 East Lake crime analysis conducted by Purpose Built Communities using Atlanta Police Department data accessible at http://www .atlantapd.org; 1993 pre-revitalization crime data from A Chance to Succeed:

Economic Revitalization of Atlanta's East Lake Community, Selig Center for Economic Growth, Terry College of Business, University of Georgia, Fall 2008, https://www.terry.uga.edu/sites/default/files/inline-files/east_lake_study.pdf.

75. Patrick Sharkey, *Stuck in Place: Urban Neighborhoods and the End of Progress toward Racial Equality* (University of Chicago Press, 2013), 23.

76. Sharkey, *Stuck in Place*, 23.

77. Paul Grogan, "The Future of Community Development," in *Investing in What Works for America's Communities* (Federal Reserve Bank of San Francisco and Low Income Investment Fund, 2012), 188.

Chapter 2. Guardrails and Airbags

1. Robert Wood Johnson Foundation Commission to Build a Healthier America, *Time to Act: Investing in the Health of Our Children and Communities*, 2014, 63.

2. D. P. Jutte, J. L. Miller, and D. J. Erickson, "Neighborhood Adversity, Child Health, and the Role for Community Development," *Pediatrics* 135, Suppl 2 (March 2015): S48–57.

3. An expanded series of city maps developed by the Robert Wood Johnson Foundation and the Virginia Commonwealth University (VCU) Center on Society and Health, https://www.rwjf.org/en/library/infographics/washington-dc-map .html.

4. Larisa Larsen and others, "Bonding and Bridging: Understanding the Relationship between Social Capital and Civic Action," *Journal of Planning Education and Research* 24 (2004): 64–77.

5. For more on RWJ's Commission to Build a Healthier America, see http://www .commissiononhealth.org/.

6. World Health Organization. Constitution of the World Health Organization as adopted by the International Health Conference, New York, June 19–22, 1946; signed on July 22, 1946, by the representatives of sixty-one states (Official Records of the World Health Organization, no. 2, p. 100) and entered into force on April 7, 1948. In Frank P. Grad, "The Preamble of the Constitution of the World Health Organization," *Bulletin of the World Health Organization: The International Journal of Public Health* 80, no. 12 (2002): 982.

7. J. M. McGinnis and W. H. Foege, "Actual Causes of Death in the United States," *Journal of the American Medical Association* 270, no. 18 (1993): 2207–12.

8. Michael Marmot, "From Black to Acheson: Two Decades of Concern with Inequalities in Health: A Celebration of the 90th Birthday of Professor Jerry Morris," *International Journal of Epidemiology* 30, no. 5 (October 2001): 1165–71, doi.org /10.1093/ije/30.5.1165.

9. *Independent Inquiry into Inequalities in Health Report*, Chairman: Sir Donald Acheson (The Stationery Office, 1998, ISBN 0 11 322173 8).

10. F. B. Fisher, "Editorial: The Results of the COMMIT Trial," *American Journal of Public Health* 85 (1995): 159–60.

11. B. L. Needham and others, "Neighborhood Characteristics and Leukocyte Telomere Length: The Multi-ethnic Study of Atherosclerosis," *Health & Place* 28 (July 2014): 167–72.

12. G. H. Brody and others, "Neighborhood Poverty and Allostatic Load in African American Youth," *Pediatrics* 134, no. 5 (November 2014): E1362–68; P. E. Gustafsson and others, "Life-Course Accumulation of Neighborhood Disadvantage and Allostatic Load: Empirical Integration of Three Social Determinants of Health Frameworks," *American Journal of Public Health* 104, no. 5 (May 2014): 904–10; S. T. Broyles and others, "Elevated C-Reactive Protein in Children from Risky Neighborhoods: Evidence for a Stress Pathway Linking Neighborhoods and Inflammation in Children," *PLoS One* 7, no. 9 (2012): e45419; N. Slopen and others, "Childhood Adversity, Adult Neighborhood Context, and Cumulative Biological Risk for Chronic Diseases in Adulthood," *Psychosomatic Medicine* 76, no. 7 (September 2014): 481–89; A. J. Schulz and others, "Associations between Socioeconomic Status and Allostatic Load: Effects of Neighborhood Poverty and Tests of Mediating Pathways," *American Journal of Public Health* 102, no. 9 (September 2012): 1706–14.

13. W. T. Boyce and others, "Genes, Environments, and Time: The Biology of Adversity and Resilience," *Pediatrics* 147, no. 2 (2021): 1–12.

14. Nancy Krieger, "Theories for Social Epidemiology in the 21st Century: An Ecosocial Perspective," *International Journal of Epidemiology* 30 (2001): 668–77.

15. John Cassel, "The Contribution of the Social Environment to Host Resistance," *American Journal of Epidemiology* 104 (1967): 108.

16. National Center for Health Statistics, Department of Health and Human Services (US), Health, United States 2011: with special feature on socioeconomic status and health. Life expectancy at age 25, by sex and education level: United States, 1996 and 2006 (cited 2012 Nov 29), http://www.cdc.gov/nchs/data/hus/2011/fig32.pdf.

17. P. Braveman and S. Egerter, "Overcoming Obstacles to Health in 2013 and Beyond," RWJF Commission to Build a Healthier America, January 1, 2013.

18. S. Leonard Syme, "Social and Economic Disparities in Health: Thoughts about Intervention," *Milbank Quarterly* 76, no. 3 (1998): 493–505, 306–7.

19. Michael Marmot and others, "Employment Grade and Coronary Heart Disease in British Civil Servants," *Journal of Epidemiology and Community Health* 3 (1978): 244–49.

20. Stanford Encyclopedia of Philosophy, "Justice, Inequality, and Health," https://plato.stanford.edu/entries/justice-inequality-health/.

21. Author interview with S. Leonard Syme, https://www.youtube.com/watch?v=eU8xTOumoQc.

22. Margery Austin Turner and Ruth Gourevitch, "How Neighborhoods Affect the Social and Economic Mobility of Their Residents," US Partnership on Mobility from Poverty, 2017.

23. Raj Chetty and Nathaniel Hendren, "The Impacts of Neighborhoods on Intergenerational Mobility I: Childhood Exposure Effects," *Quarterly Journal of Economics* 133, no. 3 (August 2018): 1107–62, doi.org/10.1093/qje/qjy007.

24. Amy Edmonds, Center on Social Disparities in Health, UCSF; Paula Braveman, MD, MPH, Center on Social Disparities in Health, UCSF; Elaine Arkin, Robert Wood Johnson Foundation; Doug Jutte, MD, MPH, Build Healthy Places Network, "How Do Neighborhood Conditions Shape Health? An Excerpt from Making the Case for Linking Community Development and Health," https://www.buildhealthyplaces.org/content/uploads/2015/09/How-Do-Neighborhood-Conditions-Shape-Health.pdf.

25. M. Beyers, "Life and Death from Unnatural Causes: Health and Social Inequality in Alameda County," The Alameda County Public Health Department, August 2008, https://acphd-web-media.s3-us-west-2.amazonaws.com/media/data-reports/social-health-equity/docs/unnatcs2008.pdf. See also Sarah Treuhaft and Allison Karpyn, *The Grocery Gap: Who Has Access to Healthy Food and Why It Matters* (PolicyLink and the Food Trust, 2010).

26. P. Gordon-Larsen and others, "Inequality in the Built Environment Underlies Key Health Disparities in Physical Activity and Obesity," *Pediatrics* 117, no. 2 (2006): 417–24.

27. Paula Braveman and others, "Housing and Health," Issue Brief No. 7, Robert Wood Johnson Foundation Commission to Build a Healthier America, 2011.

28. M. Lynch, "Poverty and School Funding: Why Low-Income Students Often Suffer," *EdWeek* blog, October 2, 2014. See also, "More Than 40% of Low-Income Schools Don't Get a Fair Share of State and Local Funds, Department of Education Research Finds," U.S. Department of Education, Office of Communication and Outreach, press release November 30, 2011.

29. D. Erickson and others, eds., *The Enduring Challenge of Concentrated Poverty in America: Case Studies from Communities across the U.S.*, The Federal Reserve System and the Brookings Institution, 2008. See also Patrick Sharkey, *Stuck in Place: Urban Neighborhoods and the End of Progress toward Racial Equality* (University of Chicago Press, 2013).

30. P.A. Braveman and S. Egerter, *Overcoming Obstacles to Health in 2013 and Beyond* (Princeton, NJ: Robert Wood Johnson Foundation Commission to Build a Healthier America, 2013).

31. P. A. Braveman and S. Egerter, *Overcoming Obstacles to Health* (Princeton, NJ: Robert Wood Johnson Foundation Commission to Build a Healthier America, 2008). See also P. A. Braveman, C. Cubbin, and S. Egerter, "Neighborhoods and Health," Issue Brief, Robert Wood Johnson Foundation Commission to Build a

Healthier America, 2011; P. A. Braveman and S. Egerter, *Overcoming Obstacles to Health* (Princeton, NJ: Robert Wood Johnson Foundation Commission to Build a Healthier America, 2008).

32. J. P. Shonkoff, W. T. Boyce, and B. S. McEwen, "Neuroscience, Molecular Biology, and the Childhood Roots of Health Disparities: Building a New Framework for Health Promotion and Disease Prevention," *JAMA* 301, no. 21 (June 3, 2009): 2252–59. For more on the Center for the Developing Child, see https://developingchild.harvard.edu/about/who-we-are/.

33. National Scientific Council on the Developing Child, "Connecting the Brain to the Rest of the Body: Early Childhood Development and Lifelong Health Are Deeply Intertwined," Working Paper No. 15.

34. Email with Carol Naughton, Purpose Built president and CEO, Monday, January 24, 2022.

35. Wendy M. Troxel and others, "Mixed Effects of Neighborhood Revitalization on Residents' Cardiometabolic Health," *American Journal of Preventive Medicine* 61, no. 5 (November 1, 2021): 683–91.

36. U.S. Department of Health and Human Services, Community Health and Economic Prosperity: Engaging Businesses as Stewards and Stakeholders—A Report of the Surgeon General (Atlanta: U.S. Department of Health and Human Services, Centers for Disease Control and Prevention, Office of the Associate Director for Policy and Strategy, 2021), 27.

37. For more details on the index, and access to the underlying data, visit https://www.diversitydatakids.org/child-opportunity-index.

38. Sharkey, *Stuck in Place*, 17.

39. Sharkey, 19 and 25.

40. Chetty and Hendren, "The Impacts of Neighborhoods." Also see Jonathan Rothwell, *Sociology's Revenge: Moving to Opportunity (MTO) Revisited* (The Brookings Institution, May 2015).

41. Jack Rosenthal, "A Tale of One City," *New York Times*, December 26, 1971, Section SM, 4.

42. Build Healthy Places Network, Prosperity Now, and Financial Health Network, "Fostering Healthy Neighborhoods: Alignment across the Community Development, Health and Financial Well-Being Sectors," https://www.buildhealthyplaces.org/content/uploads/2020/04/Fostering-Healthy-Neighborhoods-Final.pdf.

43. Amanda Kolson Hurley, "Here's a Suburban Experiment Cities Can Learn From," *Washington Post Magazine*, July 13, 2017.

44. M. Barnes, E. Matka, and H. Sullivan, "Evidence, Understanding and Complexity: Evaluation in Non-linear Systems," *Evaluation* 9 (2003): 265–84. See also Penelope Hawe, "Lessons from Complex Interventions to Improve Health," *American Review of Public Health* 36 (2015): 307–23.

45. For a good overview of complex adaptive systems, see Melanie Mitchell, *Complexity: A Guided Tour* (Oxford University Press, 2009).

46. Barnes, Matka, and Sullivan, "Evidence, Understanding and Complexity," 265–84. See also Hawe, "Lessons from Complex Interventions," 307–23.

47. Robert Putnam, *Our Kids: The American Dream in Crisis* (New York: Simon & Schuster, 2015), 210. The trends on drug use can be found in the Drug Enforcement Agency's annual national survey of drug usage among American teens.

48. Putnam, 190 and 216.

49. Mark Granovetter, "The Strength of Weak Ties," *American Journal of Sociology* 78 (May 1973): 1360–80.

50. Ron Haskins and Isabel Sawhill, "Work and Marriage: The Way to End Poverty and Welfare," Brookings Policy Brief, September 2003.

51. Betty Hart and Todd R. Risley, *Meaningful Differences in the Everyday Experiences of Young American Children* (Baltimore: Paul H. Brooks Publishing Co, 1995).

52. There is now a debate about these findings, but they are in line with other research that shows how nurture can become nature in terms of limiting brain development and language acquisition. See https://www.edutopia.org/article/new-research-ignites-debate-30-million-word-gap#:~:text=In%20the%201990s%2C%20researchers%20Betty,than%20for%20lower%2Dincome%20children. A very interesting first-of-its-kind program, Baby's First Years, is attempting to identify the causal connections from cash payments to reduce poverty on brain development and other child development issues. See Alla Katsnelson, "A Novel Effort to See How Poverty Affects Young Brains: An Emerging Branch of Neuroscience Asks a Question Long on the Minds of Researchers: Recent Stimulus Payments Make the Study More Relevant," The Upshot, *New York Times*, April 7, 2021. "None of us thinks income is the only answer," said Dr. Kimberly Noble, a neuroscientist and pediatrician at Teachers College, Columbia University, who is co-leading the work. "But with Baby's First Years, we are moving past correlation to test whether reducing poverty directly causes changes in children's cognitive, emotional and brain development."

53. Perry Preschool 40-year follow-up: L. J. Schweinhart and others, *Lifetime Effects: The HighScope Perry Preschool Study through Age 40*, Monographs of the HighScope Educational Research Foundation, 14 (Ypsilanti, MI: HighScope Press).

   Abecedarian: F. A. Campbell and others, "Early Childhood Education: Young Adult Outcomes from the Abecedarian Project," *Applied Developmental Science* 6, no. 1 (2002): 42–57.

   Chicago Child–Parent Centers: A. J. Reynolds and others, "Long-Term Effects of an Early Childhood Intervention on Educational Achievement and Juvenile Arrest: A 15-Year Follow-up of Low-Income Children in Public Schools," *JAMA* 285, no. 18 (2001): 2339–46.

54. E. E. Werner and R. S. Smith, *Overcoming the Odds: High-Risk Children from Birth to Adulthood* (Ithaca, NY: Cornell University Press, 1992).

55. For more on Outward Bound, see https://www.outwardbound.org/.

56. For more information on this program, see https://ccc.ca.gov/.

57. Penelope Douglas and David Erickson, "CultureBank: A New Paradigm for Community Investment," March 2017, Working Paper 2017-01.

58. For the full transcript of Martin Luther King Jr.'s "The Drum Major Instinct" sermon, see https://kinginstitute.stanford.edu/king-papers/documents/drum -major-instinct-sermon-delivered-ebenezer-baptist-church.

59. M. J. Poulin, "Volunteering Predicts Health among Those Who Value Others: Two National Studies," *Health Psychology* 33, no. 2 (2014): 120–29, doi.org/10 .1037/a0031620.

60. Klaus Schmidt, "Zuerst kam der Tempel, dann die Stadt," Vorläufiger Bericht zu den Grabungen am Göbekli Tepe und am Gürcütepe 1995–1999," *Istanbuler Mitteilungen* 50 (2000): 5–41. As the title of this article in German says, "First came the temple, then the city."

61. T. S. Elliot, "Little Gidding," http://www.columbia.edu/itc/history/winter /w3206/edit/tseliotlittlegidding.html.

62. Alexi Jones, "Reforms without Results: Why States Should Stop Excluding Violent Offenses from Criminal Justice Reforms," Press Release. Prison Policy Initiative. Assessment based on data from the Federal Bureau of Investigation, Crime in the United States 2018 Table 38 and U.S. Census Bureau, Annual Estimates of the Resident Population by Single Year of Age and Sex for July 1, 2018.

63. Patrick Sharkey, "Two Lessons of the Urban Crime Decline," *New York Times*, January 13, 2018.

64. REDF, "Impact Highlights," https://redf.org/about/our-story/.

65. David H. Autor, "Skills, Education, and the Rise of Earnings Inequality among the 'Other 99 Percent,'" *Science* 344, no. 6186 (May 23, 2014): 843–51.

66. For more background on Lyra Health, see https://www.lyrahealth.com/.

67. For more information on Unite US, see https://uniteus.com/.

Chapter 3. Financing Guardrails and Airbags

1. This phrase was first coined by Kevin Jones, cofounder of the Social Capital Markets (SOCAP) conference.

2. Adam Smith, *The Essential Adam Smith* (W.W. Norton, 1987), 323.

3. H. Luke Shaefer, Kate Naranjo, and David Harris, "Spending on Government Anti-poverty Efforts: Healthcare Expenditures Vastly Outstrip Income Transfers," Poverty Solutions, University of Michigan, October 18, 2019.

4. Laurie Goodman, Jun Zhu, and John Walsh, *The Community Reinvestment Act: What Do We Know, and What Do We Need to Know?* Working paper (Urban Institute, 2019).

5. Douglas Jutte, "The Role of Community Development as a Partner in Health," in *The Practical Playbook: Public Health and Primary Care Together*, ed. J. Lloyd Michener and others, chap. 35.

6. R. L. Thornton and others, "Evaluating Strategies for Reducing Health Disparities by Addressing the Social Determinants of Health," *Health Affairs* 35, no.8 (August 1, 2016): 1416–23, doi:10.1377/hlthaff.2015.1357.

7. Jacqueline LaPointe, "How Addressing Social Determinants of Health Cuts Healthcare Costs," Xtelligent Healthcare Media.

8. Centers for Medicare & Medicaid Services, "Accountable Health Communities Model," available at: https://innovation.cms.gov/innovation-models/ahcm.

9. Centers for Medicare & Medicaid Services, "RE: Value-Based Care Opportunities in Medicaid," SMD# 20-004, December 21, 2020, 4.

10. Centers for Medicare & Medicaid Services, "Accountable Health Communities: Evaluation of Performance Years 1–3 (2017–2020)."

11. LaPointe, "How Addressing Social Determinants."

12. The Commonwealth Fund, "Welcome to the Return on Investment (ROI) Calculator for Partnerships to Address the Social Determinants of Health," https://www.commonwealthfund.org/roi-calculator?redirect_source=/welcome-roi-calculator.

13. Brian Castrucci and John Auerbach, "Meeting Individual Social Needs Falls Short of Addressing Social Determinants of Health," *Health Affairs Forefront* (blog), January 16, 2019.

14. Castrucci and Auerbach.

15. Leora I. Horwitz and others, "Quantifying Health Systems' Investment in Social Determinants of Health, by Sector, 2017–19," *Health Affairs* 39, no. 2 (February 2020): 192–98, Opioids, Investing in Social Determinants & More, doi:10.1377/hlthaff.2019.01246. For a survey of how hospital systems have been investing in grocery stores as a way to improve health, see Build Healthy Places, "Healthcare Systems Back Grocery Stores in Food Deserts: Access to Healthy Food Can Support Not Only Personal Health but Neighborhood Health," November 17, 2020.

16. Becker's Hospital Review, "100 Integrated Health Systems to Know."

17. Centers for Medicare & Medicaid Services, "National Health Expenditures Fact Sheet."

18. Centers for Medicare & Medicaid Services, "NHE Summary, Including Share of GDP, CY 1960–2019."

19. Jme McLean and Tyler Norris, "Building a Market for Health: Achieving Community Outcomes through a Total Health Business Model," in *What Matters: Investing in Results to Build Strong, Vibrant Communities* (Federal Reserve Bank of San Francisco and the Nonprofit Finance Fund, 2017), 175.

20. National Academies of Sciences, Engineering, and Medicine, *Communities in Action: Pathways to Health Equity* (Washington, DC: The National Academies

Press, 2017); J. P. Shonkoff and others, "Leveraging the Biology of Adversity and Resilience to Transform Pediatric Practice," *Pediatrics* 147, no. 2 (2021): e20193845.

21. *What Matters: Investing in Results to Build Strong, Vibrant Communities* (San Francisco: Federal Reserve Bank of San Francisco and the Nonprofit Finance Fund, 2017).

22. Andrea Levere, "The Measures of a Movement: Investing for Results Now and Tomorrow," in *What Matters: Investing in Results to Build Strong, Vibrant Communities* (Federal Reserve Bank of San Francisco, 2017), 456.

23. John Olson and Andrea Phillips, "Rikers Island: The First Social Impact Bond in the United States," *Community Development Innovation Review* 9, no. 1 (April 2013): 97.

24. Donald Cohen and Jennifer Zelnick, "What We Learned from the Failure of the Rikers Island Social Impact Bond," *Nonprofit Quarterly*, August 7, 2015.

25. Stephen Goldsmith, "Utah Applies Social Impact Bonds to Early Childhood Education: The Investment Tool Is Catching on as a Better, Safer Way to Invest Scarce Public Resources," *Governing*, February 18, 2015.

26. Amanda Abrams, "Better, Faster, Cheaper Ways to Finance Supportive Housing: A Few Cities in the U.S. Are Addressing Homelessness by Experimenting with Different Financing Vehicles That Are Helping to Preserve and Construct More Supportive Housing," *Shelterforce*, December 16, 2021.

27. The longitude inducements were a prize-based award established in 1714. It was granted to whomever could solve the technical problem of determining a ship's longitude at sea. For more, see the Papers of the Board of Longitude at http://cudl.lib.cam.ac.uk/collections/rgo14/1.

28. Christopher Frangione, Jennifer Bravo, and Stephanie Wander, "The Power of Incentive Prize Competitions," in *What Matters*, 210.

29. Andrew Levitt and Lara Metcalf, "Outcomes Rate Cards: A Path to Paying for Success at Scale," in *What Matters*, 242.

30. David James Erickson, *The Housing Policy Revolution: Networks and Neighborhoods* (Washington DC: Urban Institute Press, 2009), 86–88.

31. For details on how the Low-Income Housing Tax Credit works, see Erickson, *Housing Policy Revolution*.

32. Terri Ludwig, "Can the Housing Tax Credit Be a Model for Connecting Capital to More Human-Centered Outcomes?" in *What Matters*, 220.

33. For more on the IRS Form 8609, see https://www.irs.gov/forms-pubs/about-form -8609.

34. Maggie Super Church, "Investing in Health from the Ground Up: Building a Market for Healthy Neighborhoods," in *What Matters*, 273.

35. Nancy O. Andrews and Janis Bowdler, "Equity with a Twist: Getting to Outcomes With Flexible Capital," in *What Matters*, 258.

36. Kimberlee Cornett, "The Strong Families Fund: Outcomes-Driven Resident Service Coordination," in *What Matters*, 202.

37. Emily Gustafsson-Wright, "Performance-Based Contracting Can Provide Flexibility, Drive Efficiency, and Focus Resources on What Works in Social Services," in *What Matters*, 56.

38. The typology of this market into "buyers of health," "producers," and "connectors" was developed by Ian Galloway, Federal Reserve Bank of San Francisco, for the SOCAP Health Conference in 2013. For more details on that conference, see the agenda and other content at http://www.frbsf.org/community-development /events/2013/september/socap-social-capital-markets-health/.

39. For an extensive discussion of how "control of destiny" can improve health, see the following interview with S. Leonard Syme: https://www.youtube.com/watch ?v=eU8xTOumoQc.

40. Claire Cain Miller, "Why the New Monthly Child Tax Credit Is More Likely to Be Spent on Children," The Upshot, *New York Times*, July 16, 2021.

41. The Community Development Trust website: https://cdt.biz/about-us/history/.

42. Afdhel Aziz, "How Nico, a Benefit Company, Is Using Fractional Ownership to Help Local Communities Share in Real Estate Success," *Forbes*, August 5, 2020.

43. David Zuckerman, "Hospitals Building Healthier Communities: Embracing the Anchor Mission," Democracy Collaborative, March 2013, https://community -wealth.org/sites/clone.community-wealth.org/files/downloads/Zuckerman -HBHC-2013.pdf.

44. Steven Ross Johnson, "Hospitals Pledge $700 Million to Fight Economic Social Disparities," *Modern Healthcare*, November 5, 2019. Also, see an announcement directly from the Healthcare Anchor Network itself: https://healthcareanchor .network/2019/11/health-system-leaders-announce-over-700-million-in -investments-to-address-health-housing-economic-inequalities-through -community-wealth-building/.

45. U.S. Department of Health and Human Services, *Community Health and Economic Prosperity: Engaging Businesses as Stewards and Stakeholders—a Report of the Surgeon General* (Atlanta: U.S. Department of Health and Human Services, Centers for Disease Control & Prevention, Office of the Associate Director for Policy and Strategy).

46. For more information on the State Innovation Models (SIM) initiative, see https://innovation.cms.gov/innovation-models/state-innovations.

47. Len Nichols and others, "Collaborative Approach to Public Goods Investments (CAPGI): Lessons Learned from a Feasibility Study," August 13, 2020.

48. Rebecca Nielsen, David Muhlestein, and Michael Leavitt, "Social Determinants of Health: Aggregated Precision Investment," June 14, 2021.

49. Geographic Direct Contracting Model, Centers for Medicare & Medicaid Services (CMS), and Center for Medicare and Medicaid Innovation (Innovation Center):

https://innovation.cms.gov/innovation-models/geographic-direct-contracting -model.

50. Nancy E. Adler, "Assessing Health Effects of Community Development," in *Investing in What Works for America's Communities* (San Francisco: Federal Reserve Bank of San Francisco and the Low Income Investment Fund, 2012), 275.

51. For more details on Project Welcome Home, see https://www.sccgov.org/sites/osh /solutions/SpecialInitiatives/Pages/Project-Welcome-Home.aspx.

52. "Attributable risk (AR) is the portion of disease rate attributable to the exposure factor in the epidemiological context, the portion of correct diagnosis rate attributable to a positive predictive result (e.g., lab test) in the clinical context, or the portion of beneficial outcome rate attributable to a treatment." Robert H. Riffenburgh and Daniel L. Gillen, *Statistics in Medicine*, 4th ed. (Oxford: Academic Press, 2020), 215.

53. jon a. powell, Stephen Menendian, and Wendy Ake, "Targeted Universalism: Policy & Practice: A Primer," Haas Institute for a Fair and Inclusive Society, May 8, 2019.

54. Elizabeth Kneebone and Emily Garr, *Suburbanization of Poverty: Trends in Metropolitan America, 2000 to 2008*, Metropolitan Opportunity Series (Metropolitan Policy Program at Brookings, January 2010).

55. Antony Bugg-Levine, "So, Why All This Fuss about Results and Outcomes?" in *What Matters: Investing in Results to Build Strong, Vibrant Communities*, 25.

56. Chester Hartman, "Feeding the Sparrows by Feeding the Horses," *Shelterforce* 14, no. 1 (1992): 12–15; David James Erickson, *The Housing Policy Revolution: Networks and Neighborhoods* (Urban Institute, 2009), 92.

57. This was a comment onstage by Shonkoff at the Federal Reserve System Community Development Research Conference (Washington, DC, March 23–24, 2017). More information is available at https://minneapolisfed.org/community/tenth-biennial -federal-reserve-system-community-development-research-conference/agenda.

58. David Brooks, "The Future of the American Left," *New York Times*, May 3, 2018, A23.

59. Jodi Halpern and Douglas Jutte, "The Ethics of Outcomes-Based Funding Models," in *What Matters: Investing in Results to Build Strong, Vibrant Communities* (San Francisco: Federal Reserve Bank of San Francisco and the Nonprofit Finance Fund, 2017), 410.

60. David Erickson, *Housing Policy Revolution: Networks and Neighborhoods* (Urban Institute, 2009).

61. Doris Kearns Goodwin, *Team of Rivals* (New York: Simon & Schuster, 2005), 90.

Chapter 4. Hawaii Case Study

1. Adam Smith, *An Inquiry into the Nature and Causes of the Wealth of Nations*, edited by R. H. Campbell and A. S. Skinner (Indianapolis: Liberty Press, 1981), 418–19.

2. Nationwide Children's, Partners for Kids, more available at https://www .nationwidechildrens.org/impact-quality/partners-for-kids-pediatric-account able-care.

3. Elizabeth Hinton and others, "A First Look at North Carolina's Section 1115 Medicaid Waiver's Healthy Opportunities Pilots," May 15, 2019.

4. Rose Hoban, *North Carolina Health News*, "Health Insurance Premium Picture for Coming Year Uncertain," July 28, 2020.

5. Elise Reuter, "CityBlock, a Primary Care Startup Focused on Underserved Communities, Passes $1 Billion Valuation," *MedCity News*, December 10, 2020. Reuter writes, "CityBlock provides care for patients covered by Medicaid and dual-eligible patients, who are covered by both Medicare and Medicaid. It strikes value-based contracts with insurers in the markets where it currently operates, which include New York, Massachusetts, Connecticut and Washington D.C." More details are available at https://medcitynews.com/2020/12/cityblock-a-primary-care-startup -focused-on-underserved-communities-passes-1-billion-valuation/.

6. US Census, "Hawaii Population Characteristics 2019," June 25, 2020, 4.

7. Available at http://dbedt.hawaii.gov/economic/ranks/.

8. This map was created using the tool provided by the Center for Applied Research and Engagement Systems, or CARES, at the University of Missouri.

9. "Cost-of-Living Adjusted Wage Data for U.S. Metro Areas," *Governing*, February 25, 2015.

10. United Way of Hawaii, "ALICE in Hawai'i: A Financial Hardship Study," 2020, ii.

11. US Census, "Quick Facts: Hawaii." The national poverty rate is at a historic low. Jessica Semega and others, "Income and Poverty in the United States: 2019," revised September 2021, US Census.

12. "Real Personal Income for States and Metropolitan Areas 2013," U.S. Dept. of Commerce Bureau of Economic Analysis, July 1, 2015.

13. For more information, see Kathleen S. Short, "The Supplemental Poverty Measure: Examining the Incidence and Depth of Poverty in the U.S. Taking Account of Taxes and Transfers in 2012," U.S. Census Bureau, November 20, 2013; Liana Fox, "The Supplemental Poverty Measure: 2018," October 2019. Table A-5, Number and Percentage of People in Poverty by State, 28.

14. Andrew Aurand and others, "Out of Reach: 2020," National Low Income Housing Coalition.

15. "State of Homelessness: 2020 Edition," National Alliance to End Homelessness.

16. Food Security in the U.S.: Key Statistics and Graphs, U.S. Department of Agriculture, www.ers.usda.gov/topics/food-nutrition-assistance/food-security-in -the-us/key-statisticsgraphics.aspx.

17. S. A. Berkowitz and others, "State-Level and County-Level Estimates of Health Care Costs Associated with Food Insecurity," *Preventing Chronic Disease* 16 (2019): 180549, doi:10.5888/pcd16.180549; Table 2, Estimates of Health Care

Costs Associated with Food Insecurity, by US State, Using Food Insecurity Prevalence, United States, 2016 from Map the Meal Gap Data.

18. Berkowitz and others, "State-Level and County-Level Estimates of Health Care Costs."

19. United Health Foundations, "America's Health Rankings," https://www.americas healthrankings.org/explore/annual/measure/Obesity/state/HI.

20. Nathan Eagle, "Hawai'i Youth Suicide Rate Doubles in 5 Years," Hawai'i Civil Beat, October 26, 2012.

21. United Health Foundations, "America's Health Rankings."

22. Hawaii State Department of Health, "Drug Overdose Deaths among Hawaii Residents, 1999–2014," http://www.hawaiihealthmatters.org/content/sites/hawaii /2015_Hawaii_Drug_Overdose_Death_Special_Emphasis_Report_2015.pdf.

23. Hawai'i Appleseed Center for Law and Economic Justice, "State of Poverty in Hawai'i," April 2016, 20.

24. US Census, "Quick Facts," https://www.census.gov/quickfacts/fact/table/los angelescountycalifornia,CA/PST045219.

25. US Census, "Quick Facts," https://www.census.gov/quickfacts/mauicountyhawaii.

26. Robert Frank, "Top States for Millionaires Per Capita," CNBC, January 15, 2014.

27. Urban Institute, National Center of Charitable Statistics, "Registered 501(c)(3) Private Foundations by State."

28. "Report on Financial Activities July 1, 2016–June 30, 2017," Kamehameha Schools, June 30, 2017.

29. Hawaii News Now, "Hawaiian Word of the Day: Kuleana," April 17, 2015.

30. Email exchange with Raymond Fong, Vice President, Strategic Market Planning & Analytics, Kaiser Permanente, August 8, 2022.

31. Kimberly Miyazawa Frank, DHS Director of Community Development, "The History of 'Ohana Nui: Transformation of the Department of Human Services," August 2018.

32. Frank, 7.

33. Judy Mohr Peterson, "Hawaii's Vision for Health Care Transformation: Hawai'i 'Ohana Nui Project Expansion (HOPE) Program," 5.

34. Peterson.

35. For more on Opportunity Zones, see the Urban Institute and Brookings Institution Tax Policy Center, https://www.taxpolicycenter.org/briefing-book/what -are-opportunity-zones-and-how-do-they-work.

36. The Early Childhood Action Strategy (ECAS).

37. Early Childhood Action Strategy Org Chart and Network Structure.

38. Kumu, "Waianae Alliance Map." For more information on Kumu and how this tool can help map complex adaptive systems, see https://hiqol.kumu.io/hawaii -quality-of-life.

39. More information on MaʻO Organic Farms can be found at www.maoorganicfarms .org/.

40. Maʻo Organic Farms, "2019 Growth & Impact Report."

41. Hawaii State Department of Education, "ʻAina Pono Programs."

42. Maria Kanai, "Food for Thought: Hawaiʻi's Public School Lunches Are Chang-ing in a Big Way," *Honolulu Magazine*, May 30, 2019.

43. State of Hawaii Office of Planning, "Increased Food Security and Food Self-Sufficiency Strategy: A State Strategic/Functional Plan," October 2012, ii.

44. For more background on John Cassel, see chapter 3 and https://epiresearch.org /john-cassel/.

45. Kōkua Kalihi Valley.

46. Waianae Coast Comprehensive Health Center.

47. Polynesian Voyaging Society.

48. Polynesian Voyaging Society.

49. Hawaii Community Foundation, "Connect for Success."

50. Hawaii Community Foundation, "Pathways to Resilient Communities."

51. The Council for Native Hawaiian Advancement (CNHA).

52. Krista A. Jahnke, "Mission, Money & Markets: Kresge Supports the Efforts of Native Hawaiians to Topple Barriers to Home Ownership," *General Foundation News*, September 5, 2018.

53. "CDFIs in Hawaii," CDFI Coalition.

54. Housing ASAP Fact Sheet.

55. Hawaiian Data Collaborative.

56. Ashish Abraham, President, Foresight Health Solutions, "Developing a New Ar-tificial Intelligence-Driven Care Coordination Paradigm in Hawaii," North-west Regional Primary Care Association, April 4, 2022, available at https://www .nwrpca.org/news/601248/Developing-a-New-Artificial-Intelligence-Driven -Care-Coordination-Paradigm-in-Hawaii.htm.

57. Foresight Health Solutions, https://foresighthealthsolutions.com/.

Chapter 5. Conclusion and Next Steps

1. Anna Bezanson, "The Early Use of the Term Industrial Revolution," *Quarterly Journal of Economics* 36, no. 2 (February 1922): 343–49.

2. For more on this idea, please see Nathaniel Counts and others, "The Needs for New Cost Measures in Pediatric Value-Based Payment," *Pediatrics* 147, no. 2 (February 2021): e20194037.

3. Jan de Vries, *The Industrious Revolution: Consumer Behavior and the Household Economy, 1650 to the Present* (Cambridge University Press, 2008).

4. Pablo Neruda, Nobel Lecture, December 13, 1971, "Towards the Splendid City."

Index

Figures are indicated by "f" following page numbers.

Bagehot, Walter, 119
Baker, Dean, 116
Baltimore: Empowerment Zones in, 48;
    Johnston Square neighborhood of, 58;
    Living Cities Integration Initiative in,
    55; Rebuild Metro in, 58
Banks: Community Reinvestment Act
    requirements for, 41, 43–45, 131, 139;
    in Hawaii, 131, 139; redlining practices
    of, 41, 43, 44*f*
Bedford Stuyvesant Restoration Corpora-
    tion, 40
Behavior, as factor in good health, 65–66
Biden administration, 55, 107
Black Report (1980), 65
Blacks: in Hawaii, 122; life expectancy
    trends for, 9; in low opportunity
    neighborhoods, 74, 75; redlining
    practices affecting, 41, 43
Blockchain technology, 2, 91, 111, 150
Bloomberg Foundation, 102
Boston: economic mobility in, 15, 16*f*, 17;
    population trends in, 47
Boyce, Tom, 18
Boy Scouts, 83
Bradley, Elizabeth H., 9, 18
Bravata, Dena, 89
Braveman, Paula, 70
Breadlines in depression era, 36, 36*f*
Brophy, Paul, 58, 60
Bugg-Levine, Antony, 115
Build Healthy Communities Initiative, 56
Bullying, 1–2
Burnham, Daniel, 78
Bush administration, 49
Buyers of health, 26–27, 100, 106–7, 110;
    federal government as, 100; in Hawaii,
    31, 32, 128–31; impact of cash flow
    from, 145; in transition to new system,
    145, 147, 148. *See also* connectors

California: Civilian Conservation Corp in,
    83; economic mobility in, 15, 16*f*, 17;
    HOPE SF program in, 56; Project
    Welcome Home in, 111, 150; wall
    mural project in, 84
California Endowment, 27, 50, 56

Callahan, David, 17
Camden, Empowerment Zones in, 48
Capital: access of low-income communities
    to, 43–46; and economy of historical
    Northern Europe, 119; in Industrial
    Revolution, 146–47; social, and
    economic mobility, 17
Capital stacks created by CDFIs, 105,
    140
Capitation, 26, 97
Cardiovascular disease, 71, 72
Caretakers, nonparent, as producers of
    health, 28
Cassel, John, 66–67, 137
Castrucci, Brian, 98–99
Catcher in the Rye, 2
CDFIs. *See* community development
    financial institutions
Centers for Disease Control and Preven-
    tion, 87, 125
Centers for Medicare and Medicaid
    Services, 97–98, 100, 109
Cermak, Anton, 36
Chapman, Tracy, 66
Charlotte, economic mobility in, 15, 16*f*, 17
Chetty, Raj, 17, 70, 75, 87
Chicago: Empowerment Zones in, 48;
    population trends in, 47
Chicago Child–Parent Centers, 82
Childhood: adverse experiences in, 71, 130;
    fifth freedom in, 1–2, 152; in high
    opportunity neighborhoods, 73;
    language development in, 82; in low
    opportunity neighborhoods, 70, 73–74;
    parent spending on enrichment
    resources during, 23, 24*f. See also*
    education; kindergarten readiness
Child Opportunity Index, 74, 88–89
Child Tax Credit, 107
Choice Neighborhoods program, 51–52, 55
Chronic disease: as downstream problem,
    18, 19, 34; health expenditures on, 18,
    71, 94
Cincotta, Gail, 43
CityBlock Health, 121
City Health Dashboard, 87
Civilian Conservation Corp, 83

Civil service employees, Whitehall study on health outcomes for, 67–69, 69*f*
Civil War era, 34
Cleveland: economic mobility in, 15, 16*f*; Living Cities Integration Initiative in, 55; population trends in, 47
Clinton administration, 47–48, 49
Cognitive skills, neighborhood opportunities affecting, 75
Collaborative Approach to Public Good Investments, 109
Collaborative Governance for Urban Revitalization (Rich & Stoker), 47
Collective Impact model of FSG Consulting, 21–22, 51, 55
College education, economic consequences of, 86
Columbus OH, 121
Commonwealth Fund, 98
Community action agencies, 39, 40
Community-based organizations, 96
Community Commons, 88
Community development block grants, 41, 45, 46, 96, 131
Community development corporations, 39–41, 42, 96
Community development financial institutions (CDFIs), 40–41, 42, 43, 45, 96; capital stacks created by, 105, 140; as connectors, 108, 139–40; in Hawaii, 139–40; and outcomes-based financing, 105
Community Development Trust, 107–8
Community entrepreneurs, 105, 112, 113, 114; as producers of health, 28
Community Health and Economic Prosperity, 109
Community institutions and activities as social guardrails, 71
Community involvement, 22; in collective impact model, 21–22; in Promise Neighborhoods, 53; in Purpose Built Communities, 59; in Rebuild Metro, 58
Community loan funds, 40
Community needs: collective impact model on, 21–22; recipe thinking on, 21;

regional differences in, 113; social guardrails and airbags in, 23–26
Community Reinvestment Act (1977), 41, 43–45; annual amount invested under, 45, 94; in Hawaii, 131, 139
Complex adaptive systems, 78–80, 116, 150; in Hawaii, 134
Comprehensive Community Initiatives, 57
Connecting for Success program in Hawaii, 138
Connectors, 110–11; demand pressures affecting, 145; examples of, 107–8; in Hawaii, 32, 138–42; Pay for Success strategies as, 28–29, 107; role in market valuing health, 26, 28–30
Consumers of health. *See* buyers of health
Control of destiny: community sense of, 117; and health outcomes, 67–69; producers of health in, 107
Cornett, Kimberlee, 105
Cost of living in Hawaii, 124, 132
Council for Native Hawaiian Advancement, 139
COVID-19 pandemic, 9, 34
Crime: costs of victimization from, 12, 14*f*; violent, rate of, 85
Criminal justice system, 85; bias in, 81; downstream expenditures on, 12, 14*f*, 19; and employment of formerly convicted, 81, 86; and social impact bond on juvenile recidivism, 102–03

Data collection and analysis, 86–91, 150; artificial intelligence in, 141–42, 150; blockchain technology in, 91, 111, 150; in Hawaii, 32, 134, 141–42; privacy in, 91, 111; in Project Welcome Home, 111; by Unite US, 90, 91, 111
Deep poverty, 5–6, 14
Demand pressures, 145, 149–50; from buyers of health, 128, 131; in community development funding, 42; for market valuing health, 94, 95, 96–97, 128, 131; outcomes-based financing in, 106; on producers of health, 148; in quasi-markets, 42, 95; Smith on, 93–94; technology innovations in, 150